Intercultural Communication in Business:

How Context and Other Cultural Factors Affect Communication in Multicultural Organizations

By Kelly Nix, DBA

Intercultural Communication in Business
By Kelly Nix

©2015, Kelly Nix
San Antonio, Texas 78250

ISBN-13: 978-1506145334
ISBN-10: 1506145337

Dedication

To my wife, Valerie, who for nearly three years saw me glued to the computer, but whose love and support kept me going; to my parents, Robert and Sue Nix, who brought me into an intercultural world and instilled in me from an early age a deep respect for people of all ethnicities and cultural backgrounds; to my in-laws, Vicente and Julia Garcia, for their tireless support; to Theresa Spicer, an exceptional academic mentor in my undergraduate program without whom my dream of pursuing a doctorate might well have withered on the vine; to my supervisors and colleagues, to the ministers of Iglesia Cristiana Apostólica del Perú and other study volunteers for making this research possible; to the faculty of California InterContinental University, for their constant encouragement and inspiration; and, most importantly, to Jesus Christ, through whom I can do all things.

Acknowledgements

Special thanks to my academic mentors, Dr. Fathiah Inserto and Dr. Amarjit Singh; to Dr. Kamalnayan Inamdar and the members of the Graduate Review Committee at California InterContinental University; and in particular to Dr. Raymond Briggs for his technical guidance in the area of statistical analysis.

Preface

This study was originally conducted in 2011 as the capstone of my doctoral program, in which I was tasked to apply existing knowledge to a real-life business problem. It so happened that the organization with which I was employed at the time was experiencing a real struggle with internal communication due to its international and multicultural composition. I found the results of the study to be fascinating, and I have made them available to the public in hopes that they will be of help to companies and organizations of all types who face similar challenges in communication.

Abstract

This study examines the effects of national culture on business communications. It is set in what is referred to throughout the document as "Organization A," a multinational child sponsorship non-profit based in the United States and operating in 11 countries worldwide. An extensive review of the existing literature is presented, where cultural aspects such as collectivism and individualism, high and low context in culture, monochronism and polychronism, etc., are examined in detail. Exploratory research is conducted on the experientially based premise that national culture does indeed have a significant effect on how business communication is perceived and decoded, and that different national cultures will approach collectivism and individualism, conflict avoidance, and task- versus people-orientation differently. The results of the investigation within Organization A were consistent with this position. Finally, suggestions for future research are offered that might quantitatively test and validate the premise. A communications guidebook is created for use within Organization A.

Table of Contents

Tables Used

Figures Used

Intercultural Communication in Business:

How Context and Other Cultural Factors Affect Communication in Multicultural Organizations

By Kelly Nix, DBA

Chapter 1: Introduction and Problem Statement

This document proposes to build upon established research on high-context (HC) and low-context (LC) cultures to examine the effects of these cultural aspects on business communication. While a significant amount of research has been conducted on the subject of communication within HC and LC cultures (Gudykunst, 1997; Hofstede, 1980; Martin, Hammer & Bradford, 1994), much of this research addresses intercultural communication at a general level. The purpose of this document is to more closely examine how context and other cultural factors influence internal business communication (specifically, electronic communication) within the narrow focus of a multinational, multicultural organization.

Background

At the time this study was conducted, the author served as a functional, U.S.-based supervisor to a team of 16 international field correspondents located in 11 countries in North America, Central America, South America, the Caribbean, Africa, and Asia, for a multi-national, non-profit child sponsorship organization, known throughout this study as Organization A. The field correspondents, known as communications coordinators (CCs), were distributed as follows; Chile (1), Colombia (2), Ecuador (2), Dominican Republic (1), Guatemala (1), Honduras (1), India (1), Mexico (1), the Philippines (4), the United States (1) and Zambia (1), creating a team marked by broad cultural diversity and geographic dispersion.

The CCs serve as in-house journalists, whose responsibilities revolve around gathering, organizing and transmitting news and story ideas to the organization's home office in the United States. The information is used by the writers, graphic artists and video producers of the Creative Services department in the entity's various publications, including a glossy magazine with three annual printings and a circulation in excess of 400,000; the organization's monthly electronic news bulletin; the company's website; marketing and sponsor acquisition collateral; and numerous smaller publications, both printed and electronic.

One of the challenges the team has constantly faced since the first CCs were hired in 2005 has been that of assignments turned in past their deadlines and frustrations in communication among and between the home office in the United States and the CCs in the field. Of the U.S.-based writers and graphic designers who made up the team at the time of this study, only the author was fluent in both English and Spanish, the primary languages spoken by team members. Of the CCs, several in the

Americas were conversant in English, but all were more comfortable speaking and writing in Spanish. None of the CCs in Asia or Africa spoke Spanish. All the team members were educated at least to the bachelor's degree level. Several held or were pursuing graduate degrees.

Of all the countries represented on the team, only the United States is considered to have a low-context culture; all others are high-context. High-context cultures are characterized by a less linear, less direct style of communication, where the listener is expected to be able to judge the intent of the speaker by the context of what is spoken, including body language, facial expressions and tone of voice more than by the actual words spoken. In contrast, low-context cultures communicate in a very linear and direct fashion, with explicit detail ("High-context and low-context," n.d.).

Another factor to be considered in intercultural communication is how each culture views time. Samovar, Porter & McDaniel (2010) reference Hall's (1983) essay on polychronic and monochronic perceptions of time. Hall holds that people in polychronic cultures do many things simultaneously, are more concerned with people and the present moment than with schedules, and believe that they are in command of time rather than being controlled by it. In monochronic cultures, however, people organize their lives around time and emphasize schedules and promptness. All but one of the communications coordinators came from polychronic cultures, while the team at the home office in the United States was monochronic. Clearly, this may have an important bearing on the differences in perception of schedules and deadlines that have historically created tensions within the team.

Strategy of the Research Investigation

The primary research question addressed is how these contextual differences in communication from culture to culture affect electronic intercultural communications such electronic mail (email), where the receiver is unable to visually engage the sender in order to build a contextual framework to decode the message. This is especially relevant to the case at hand, as the team at the home office in the United States has a low-context communication style, but all of the communications coordinators in the field are high-context.

In order to ascertain the impact of the difference in cultural contexts on intra-team communications, exploratory instruments were developed:

- A short qualitative survey was designed where each communications coordinator was asked to identify his or her reaction to a few sample messages written in a style similar to that used for actual business communications from the home office to the field agencies. Their responses were then analyzed for clues to cultural orientation. This process was repeated with two groups not related to Organization A (referred to in this study as Group C and Group D) for additional confirmation.

- The communications coordinators and home office team members were given a task, with description limited to a bare-bones sketch of the project, a priority level and a due date. They were asked to write a small project brief assigning and explaining the task to the rest of the communications coordinators. The objective was to observe how each person approached the topics of deadlines and project instructions to ascertain what, if any, the impact of the individual's culture was on his or her communication style.

- Based on the results of the above tests, the published literature, and onsite impressions, a guidebook for intercultural communications was produced and made available to employees at the home office and in the field. The guidebook explains the concepts of high- and low-context cultures and provides recommendations for communicating clearly in an intercultural setting.

Chapter 2: Literature Review

According to Hofstede (2009), culture is more often a source of conflict than of synergy. He suggests that cultural differences are at the very least a nuisance, and are often a disaster. Storti (1994) argues that most people would not make cultural mistakes if these were obvious...but we do. No matter the culture of origin, people seem to be equally capable of sensitivity or insensitivity.

A significant amount of research has already been conducted on the effects of culture on communication. There tends to be a general consensus among investigators that culture does indeed play a significant role in correctly understanding the communicator's intent. Factors such as whether a culture is monochronic or polychronic, as well as the context (high or low) of the culture, are extremely relevant to the issue at hand in this project, which deals with the effects of culture on business communication.

No significant disagreements have been identified among the major studies reviewed by the author; all seem to agree that, while any individual within a culture may prove to be an exception to the general rule, a certain level of stereotyping is appropriate and acceptable when evaluating communication tendencies of cultures as a whole.

One significant gap in the research, however, is in the area of electronic communication (email, chat, etc.) in particular. It appears significantly fewer studies have been done on this form of intercultural communication than other more traditional means. This research project seeks to further investigate how not being able to see or (in some cases) hear the other party to a conversation affects communication between people from high- and low-context cultures.

This is of particular importance to the issue underlying this study, because the setting consists of an international team of communicators representing 11 different countries and even more cultures and subcultures. Only the team members located in the United States are culturally low-context and monochronic (with the exception of the author of this study, who is bicultural and multilingual); all other team members, who are geographically dispersed and communicate almost exclusively via email and online chat, are high-context and polychronic by culture.

Communication

According to an article in the *Concise Corsini Encyclopedia of Psychology and Behavioral Science* based on the work of Shannon and Weaver (1949) and others, interpersonal communication occurs when a source transfers information to a specific target ("Interpersonal communication," 2004). The model on which it relies applies principles of electrical engineering to human communication (see Figure 1.1):

The mind of the communicator may be considered the source of the communication. Presumably, messages originate in the brain and are encoded for transmission to other people. The source must have a means of transmitting information, such as speech, gestures, or writing. The message is encoded and sent as a signal to a receiver, who must decode the message. Thus, the destination of a message is the mind of a target or receiver person ("Interpersonal communication," 2004).

The article, "Interpersonal Communication" (2004), explains that most of these communications will typically take place in face-to-face interactions. However, they may also occur via other means such as television, telephone, mail or the Internet. Other substitutes for verbal communication may include visual contact, gestures, body orientation and the use of interpersonal space. These may also provide a context or framework in which to interpret verbal or spoken communication. Clearly, this can pose complications when communication is carried out virtually or at a distance, because the communicating parties lack the benefit of being able to observe the cues of non-verbal communication or other context.

Figure 2.1

Shannon & Weaver's (1949) Model of Human Communication

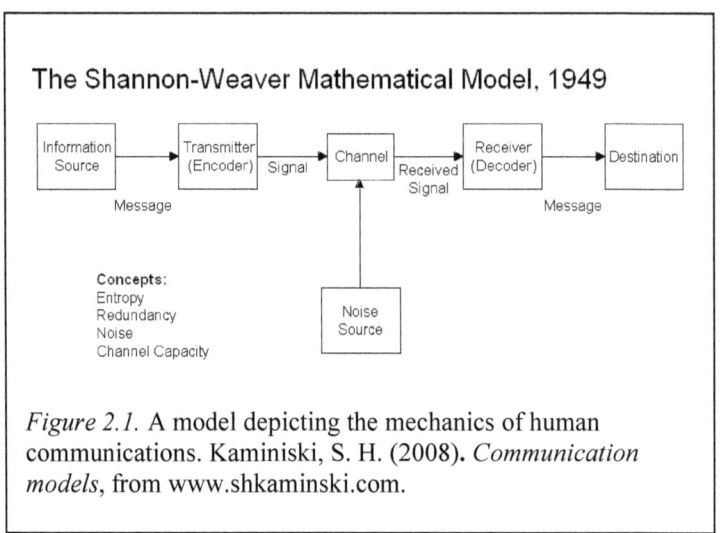

Figure 2.1. A model depicting the mechanics of human communications. Kaminiski, S. H. (2008). *Communication models*, from www.shkaminski.com.

According to an article in *World of Sociology*, communication refers to the conveyance of information, including such things as thoughts and messages, and takes place using visual signs and sounds such as language ("Communication," 2002). Chui (2011) asserts that metaphoric gestures can provide salient, additional information about the aspect of the conceptualization which is the speaker's focus of attention in real-time multimodal communication – thus underscoring the importance of visual cues to communication and, conversely, the crippling effect of the lack of these. Adding in cultural differences between the transmitter and the receiver of the communication only serves to further complicate matters. Hall (1959, 1973) declares that a non-verbal language exists not only in every country of the world, but also in various groups within each country. He affirms it is important to gain an introduction to this non-verbal language.

Definition of Culture and Its Importance to Communication

In order to properly assess the effects of culture on communication, it is first necessary to define the term "culture" for the purpose of this study. Hall (1959, 1973) paints culture as a people's way of life, or the totality of their learned behavior patterns, attitudes and material things. However, he goes on to caution that most anthropologists tend to disagree on the precise substance of culture.

Hall (1976, 1981) also describes culture as a series of situational models for behavior and thought. He argues that culture affects people's personality, the way they express themselves and show emotion, the way they think, the way they move, the way they solve problems, how they build their cities, how they plan their transportation systems, and how they put together their economic and government systems.

Trompenaars & Hampden-Turner (1998) hold to Schein's (1985) assertion that culture deals with how groups of people solve problems and reconcile dilemmas, arguing also that culture is a shared system of meanings. They further posit that culture comes in layers that must be peeled back to allow observation, revealing deeper values and norms in a society that may not be directly visible from the surface. These values affect how people approach their relationships with others, with time and with the environment.

McFarlin & Sweeney (2006) espouse Hofstede's (1993) view culture as consisting of a collective programming of people's minds, which can distinguish between two or more groups. They further agree that this cultural programming is not directly observable but can only be inferred from behavior, and that people are "often unaware of the pervasive impact of culture on their own attitudes, beliefs and behaviors." Additionally, they observe that culture is a concept that is only useful if it can accurately predict behavior, and that many cultural groups can coexist within different countries.

That culture is critical to effective communication seems clear. Communication can be classified as verbal or non-verbal, and Shi & Fan (2010) cite research by Arasaratnam & Banerjee

(2007) and Ma (1996) as evidence that failures or misunderstandings in intercultural communication are largely caused by the misinterpretation or misuse of nonverbal behaviors. Shi & Fan (2010) also refer to the findings of Lustig & Koester (2006) that "miscommunication always occurred in the understanding of nonverbal behaviors because different social contexts might create extremely different rules for appropriate and effective use of nonverbal behaviors."

Shi & Fan (2010) subscribe to the definition by DePaulo & Friedman (1998) of nonverbal communication as "the unspoken dialogue which involves the messages conveyed beyond the words." They also agree with Knapp & Hall's (2006) assertion that nonverbal communication has three major components: the communication environment, the communicators' paralinguistic characteristics and nonverbal behaviors such as body movements and positions, while concurring with Applbaum, et al (1979) that nonverbal communication is the major source of the meaning people obtain in communication.

The importance of nonverbal behavior to effective communication is of particular relevance to the subject of this study. Because members of global, intercultural and geographically-dispersed teams and work groups often communicate primarily by electronic mail, telephone or text chat, body language and other nonverbal behaviors are often indistinguishable in conversations, leaving the parties with nothing but the written or spoken word. Because of the importance of nonverbal communication and the communication environment (also referred to as context), parties to intercultural communication conducted remotely via electronic or other means are often at a disadvantage because they must process the written message with no nonverbal cues to guide them.

Cultural Identity

Jameson (2007) performs a meta-analysis of existing research on cultural identity as a foundation for an article where she hypothesizes that an expanded concept of cultural identity could help level the playing field of nationality; bring to light components specifically germane to business, such as economic class and vocational affiliation; and enhance studies in intercultural business. She examines the work of other researchers before proposing a model of cultural identity that seeks to unite social elements into a whole, allow for change as time elapses, acknowledge that elements such as power and privilege are influential, recognize the role of emotion, and associate identity with communication. She further defines cultural identity as the sense of self an individual derives from belonging, either formally or informally, to groups that transmit knowledge, beliefs, values, attitudes, traditions, and ways of life.

In relating cultural identity to communication, Jameson cites Beamer's (1995) model of intercultural communication that views audience analysis as schemata, or preexisting mental structures that allow a person to sensibly process information. The big challenge at a metacognitive level in dealing with other cultures is to know what one truly knows or does not know about others, and to reshape each of the communicator's ideas about other cultures as communication takes place.

Jameson (2007) also alludes to Victor's (1992) analysis of cross-cultural business communication as a form of ethnography in which a communicator closely observes and analyzes components of another culture. In so doing, he or she addresses seven variables that affect business communication as these variables shift in response to their cultural environment: language, environment/technology, social organization, contexting, authority, nonverbal behavior and conceptions of time. Victor asserts that if the right questions are asked about these variables, it is possible to better understand different cultures and the way they do business, and to form one's own conclusions regarding the best way to accommodate those cultural factors that may impact business-related communication with specific audiences. However, Jameson (2007) asserts that one of the most important factors in cross-cultural communication is for people to become aware of themselves and of the complexities of their own cultures, and to reflect on how these might be unlike those of people who belong to other cultures.

Jameson's (2007) hypothesis is not inconsistent with the belief of Yuan (1997) that intercultural communication theories should place more emphasis on how individuals communicate than how cultures communicate. Yuan argues that just knowing about a given culture does not necessarily mean an individual has the ability to communicate successfully with people from that culture.

Jameson (2007) contends that a weakness in much of the research done on culture is that it equates nationality with culture, ignoring key intra-national factors such as ethnicity, race, religion, class, and other components covered by more comprehensive definitions of culture, and using the terms "culture" and "country" interchangeably. She also posits that a broader concept of cultural identity could help mitigate the issue of stereotyping, which generally results from making broad-based and overly-simplified assumptions. This could be helpful in broadening the general understanding of others' multidimensional backgrounds and might discourage the assumption that a person's nationality or "race" could be more important to their cultural identity than might other factors such as class, vocation, religion and gender.

The concerns expressed by Jameson (2007) regarding overgeneralization in the application of the concept of culture could be illustrated by the common practice of regarding all Latinos as a comprehensive, unified culture under the label "Hispanic," when in reality the broad classification of Hispanic covers numerous countries, each of which possesses individual national pride and characteristics, and many of which consist of multiple and distinct sub-cultures. Therefore, future research on cultural identity should be conducted with attention to clearly defining the term "culture" and avoiding overgeneralization.

Holliday (2010) performed original research that adds a different twist to the idea of cultural identity. He surveyed 28 respondents, of which two were Australian, ten English, two Chinese, two German, one Greek, two Italian, one Mexican, two Indian, one Northern Irish, one South Korean, one Tunisian, one American, one Welsh and one Zimbabwean. The objective of his study was to explore the how people's perceptions of their cultural identity related to their nationality. The study was motivated by criticism leveled at the use of national culture to explain and predict behavior. It posed two qualitative questions: (1) What are the major features of your cultural identity? and (2) What role does nation play in this?

Some criticism can be justifiably leveled at the methodology of Holliday's (2010) study because of the limited number of respondents, their similar social statuses and their universal personal acquaintance with the researcher. Nevertheless, the general patterns that emerge from the data are interesting; Holliday was surprised to learn that his respondents violated many cultural stereotypes in that there was no evidence to indicate that Asians had types of views that differed significantly from those of Europeans, or that differences existed in cultural type, such as collectivist or individualist.

The considerable body of research that exists to substantiate the veracity of cultural factors such as collectivism or individualism (for example, the work of Hofstede (1980) casts doubt upon the validity of Holliday's (2010) study, given its multiple methodological weaknesses and marked deviations from conventional thought). Additionally, there are hints within the study that the researcher may have a politically- or ethnically-generated bias against mainstream thought on the subject. While they may have value as a curiosity or to open new areas of investigation, it seems unlikely the results of the study would hold true if extrapolated to a statistically significant sample of respondents.

General Challenges in Intercultural Communication

Following the general thread of the relationship of cultural identity to communication among cultures, Bennett (1998) argues persuasively that in order to be truly effective in intercultural communication, it is necessary to understand, appreciate and respect the idea of difference. He further posits that languages, behavior patterns, and values vary by culture, so to attempt to predict shared assumptions and responses to messages by one's own preferences and experiences is not likely to succeed. While this at first seems contradictory to Jameson's (2007) assertion that one of the most important factors in communicating across cultures is understanding oneself and one's own cultural complexities and how these might differ from those of people from other cultures, in reality both positions agree to the extent that one's cultural self-awareness is used for understanding and not prediction of intercultural responses. Bennett (1998) further suggests that in order to be interculturally competent, attention should be given to understanding subjective cultures. This also supports Jameson's (2007) position.

Bennett (1998) also emphasizes language use over linguistic structure in cross-cultural relationships, explaining that interculturalists study how nonverbal behavior, when defined by culture, can supplant or modify language; how certain communication styles express cultural ways of thinking; and how culturally-based assumptions and values can define and judge reality. This information is clearly of interest to anyone seeking to improve intercultural comprehension and communication.

Nordby (2008) holds that there is an additional dimension that must be considered when exploring the idea of intercultural communications: that of personal values and beliefs within cultures. His article hypothesizes that when those who are communicating have different values and when they fail to recognize that values that are shaped by culture differ from mere beliefs or thoughts, this can cause intercultural communication to break down. As is borne out in his article, however, this assertion is not intended to diminish the importance Nordby places on beliefs in the intercultural communication process.

To illustrate his point and emphasize the impact of beliefs on intercultural communication, Nordby (2008) uses Weihe's (2005) example of a Sami reindeer herder and a government official in Sweden who both agree that pine trees should be preserved. The fact that the reindeer herder believes in preserving the pine trees centers on the fact that his animals eat certain lichens that grow on the trees, while the government official's opinion is based on environmentalism. Therefore, although the two individuals enjoy a shared language, their agreement is based on two very different belief systems and can lead to the danger of incorrectly ascribing to each other shared beliefs. Psychologist Albert Bandura (2007, 57:50) agrees, emphasizing the importance of considering cultural values in intercultural communication.

Nordby (2008) further suggests that the term "value" is pluralistic and multifaceted; however, in one simple yet important form, values can have to do with how a person enjoys living his or her life. Coupled with the fact that people in different cultures often enjoy living their lives differently, the challenge of understanding each others' values becomes even more complex. He identifies three values-related challenges in intercultural communication: the ascription by communicators of different values to actions, differences in value conceptualization between speakers and audiences, and differences in personal values among the same, contending that these issues all differ from problems associated with language meaning and shared beliefs.

Medium-Specific Challenges in Intercultural Communication

Campbell (2008) conducted a study to prepare university students to function in global virtual teams using computer technology to facilitate intercultural communication. The specific medium chosen was electronic mail (email), which relates closely to the study at hand, as this is the primary means of communication between the home office of Organization A in the United States and the field correspondents. One of the objectives of the study was to measure the students' levels of satisfaction with email as an adequate medium for communicating interculturally.

The project consisted of 33 university students in New Zealand communicating for five weeks with 40 students in the United States. While the actual content of their discussions is not relevant to this project, their experiences with email as a medium are. The findings of the study indicated the following (Campbell 2008):

- Only 50% of students rated themselves as responding quickly to the communications of their partners
- A mere 42% felt their partners responded promptly
- Many participants disliked not being able to see their partners, their body language and physical attributes, noting that:
  - In order to truly get to know someone, on must engage in non-verbal communication, which is not possible through the Internet

- A lack of face-to-face interaction prevented participants from prompting their partners for answers, and
- When deprived of the non-verbal aspects of culture, it is impossible to achieve a thorough understanding.

Students also felt that not being able to communicate non-verbally impaired the accuracy of their interpretation of messages. Campbell (2008) indicates that all these frustrations are consistent with research by Bruning (1992); Curtis & Lawson (1999); Cheny (2001); Short, Williams, & Christie (1976); Garramone, Harris, & Anderson (n.d.); and Flaherty, Pearce, & Rubin (1998).

A Closer Look at Cultural Variability

The concept of cultural variability is crucial to understanding intercultural relations and communication. Therefore, it seems appropriate to examine the literature surrounding various dimensions of cultural variability in order to establish a basis for evaluating and improving intercultural business communication.

The concepts of cultural variability we will examine are generalizations. Storti (1994) observes that it is impossible to discuss cultures without generalizing. However, he cautions that generalizations, while perhaps accurate when referring to groups, will never be entirely true regarding individuals. This does not mean that the generalizations are incorrect; it simply means that a given trait seems to predominate within a specified culture. Notwithstanding, individuals within that culture may behave quite differently than the generalizations would suggest. Following are some important aspects of cultural variability that have been identified by cultural anthropologists. While far from exhaustive, these include individualism/collectivism, context, face, uncertainty avoidance, masculinity/femininity, harmony, concepts of time and power distance.

Individualism/Collectivism

Hofstede (2009) defines individualism – and consequently its counterpart, collectivism – as the degree to which individuals are integrated into groups. Individualist societies are characterized by loose ties between individuals, with each person responsible for looking out for him- or herself and the immediate family unit. Conversely, Hofstede asserts that people in collectivist societies are conditioned from the time they are born to integrate into in-groups that are cohesive and strong and that will protect; in return, these groups demand unquestioning loyalty. He also stresses that collectivism as a term in cultural anthropology is not political in nature, referring to the group and not the state.

Trompenaars & Hampden-Turner (1998) address the issue with a slight variation in terminology, referring to this cultural dimension as individualism and communitarianism. They agree with the assertion by Parsons & Shils (1951) that individualism involves being primarily oriented to the self, while communitarianism is gravitates primarily to shared goals and objectives, reasoning that individualistic societies seek to satisfy the desires of the individual while communitarian cultures emphasize the collective good. Cultures will typically put one or another of these orientations first in their thinking processes, although their reasoning may not necessarily exclude other approaches. Trompenaars & Hampden-Turner (1998) consider these two orientations – individualism and communitarianism – to be preferences that complement, rather than oppose, each other; they observe that the two can be reconciled by a process of integration that derives its limits from particular instances, as well as by individuals addressing the needs of the larger group of their own free will.

There is debate over the correlation between modernization and individualism. Trompenaars & Hampden-Turner (1998) cite the argument by Tönnies (1957) that the process of modernization brings societies from contexts that are very family-based and intimate with little emphasis on individualism to workplaces where tasks are individualized and differentiated according to responsibilities; they also consider the assertions of Smith (n.d.) and Weber (1947) that the division of labor has an individualizing effect that can result in dignity, autonomy, privacy and the opportunity for personal development. Trompenaars & Hampden-Turner (1998) weigh these assertions of the individualizing effect of modernization against questions exploring whether individual geniuses are the originators of new business and products, or whether the patterns of organized employees and the influence of family, teachers, friends and the community should also share the credit for such innovations.

One important consideration is that societies are continually in flux. Trompenaars & Hampden-Turner (1998) refer to French sociologist Emile Durkheim's (n.d.) nineteenth-century prediction of a future phenomenon he termed "organic solidarity" – a sophisticated form of voluntary integration among sovereign beings where individualism and communitarianism would blend to meet the changing needs of organizations and societies. Under this model, it seems reasonable that workers in multinational, multicultural organizations would trend over time toward a diminishing of their individual cultural orientations and the emergence of integrated cultures reflecting the heterogeneity and shared values of the global workplace. If this effect were to in fact be verifiable, one could expect individualistic employees in a multinational organization to gradually become more communitarian or collectivist, while communitarian employees would experience an emergence of individualistic traits.

Trompenaars & Hampden-Turner (1998) hold that varying degrees of individualism or communitarianism raise practical issues for international business. Communitarian cultures prefer plural representation in negotiations, while individualistic cultures have high esteem for the concept of individual representatives voting on behalf of their constituents according to private convictions. People of influence in individualistic cultures may be lone operators, but in communitarian cultures unaccompanied people are assumed to lack status. Anglo-Saxons expect translators in business negotiations to remain neutral, while communitarian cultures expect the translator to serve the national group as a mediator of misunderstandings that arise from culture and language. Communitarian-based decision making is typically lengthy and consultative, seeking to achieve consensus, while individualistic decision-makers may simply vote down the dissenters.

Additionally, the two dimensions are often motivated by different things; individualists tend to strive for self-actualization achieved at the top of their respective hierarchies, while communitarians may be more motivated by the idea of the respect of their fellow men. Finally, there are different perceptions of organizational structure; to the individualist, organizations tend to be viewed as instruments that have been purposefully created to serve individual owners, employees and customers, while the communitarian may view the organization as a social context that is shared by all members and which gives them meaning and purpose, serves as a family that develops and nurtures its members, and may in fact outlive them.

Interestingly, while Trompenaars & Hampden-Turner (1998) and others generally classify all of Latin America as primarily collectivist, there is divergence of opinions regarding this. Basabe & Ros (2005) cite a meta-analysis by Oyserman, Coon and Kemmelmeier (2002) that ranks Latin Americans similarly to North Americans and Western Europeans in individualism and challenges other traditional assumptions.

Yet another important subset of the concept of individualism and collectivism or communitarianism is the idea of ingroups and outgroups. Yi (2002) reviewed the work of a variety of researchers such as Altman & Taylor (1973),

Gudykunst, Yoon & Nishida (1987), Triandis (1991), and Gudykunst & Nishida (1986) on how people in different cultures interact with people in and out of their own group. A positive correlation exists between the level of collectivism in a culture and the level of synchronization and personalization within the ingroup, while cultures with high levels of individualism are quicker to trust strangers and outsiders than collectivist cultures. Due to the way management of the communications coordinators at Organization A is structured (a matrix with shared supervision coming from the home office in United States and the local agency director), ingroup bias could play an important role, as involvement from the home office (perceived as the outgroup) in prioritizing the activities of the communications coordinator (CC) at the local agency could create resentment on the part of the CC's local work team (the ingroup).

Ingroup and outgroup relationships are important because they may skew the expected effects of individualistic or collectivist culture on workgroup effectiveness, yielding surprising results. For example, Koch & Koch (2007) carried out a study in China using Hofstede's measure for individualism – collectivism that indicated groups with higher individualistic scores were more cooperative than groups that trended more collectivist. They attributed this to the fact that the individualistic groups were comprised of outgroup members, and not necessarily to inaccuracy of the basic dimensions of individualism and collectivism.

A study by Schmader & Major (1998), while not directly addressing the effects of culture on communication, nevertheless casts an interesting light on the subject at hand. They relied on the work of Crocker & Major (1989), James (1890, 1950), Rosenberg (1979), Rosenberg & Simmons (1972), Harter (1986), Pelham & Swann (1989), and Tesser & Campbell (1980) to test two hypotheses: 1) just watching how the ingroup in a particular domain performs compared to an outgroup determines how much importance or value an individual will attach to the domain, and 2) that often the measures individuals use of the performances of their fellow ingroup members serve as indicators of their own ability, and that these self-appraisals influence the way relative group performance affects selective valuing. The results proved the hypotheses correct.

The relevance of these findings to the performance of communications coordinators at Organization A has to do, again, with their unique position as matrix-managed employees who belong to two major groups: their local agency teams and the Creative Department at the home office. In a given situation, the communications coordinators might feel more affinity with one group or the other. Because of the effect of the ingroup on personal values, this could cause complications when the employee is obligated to choose between two courses of action that might be more or less beneficial to either of the ingroups, affecting the CC's ability to freely interact with, relate to and communicate with the group members.

Bos, Shami, Olson, Cheshin & Nan (2004), of the University of Michigan, conducted a study for the Computer Supported Cooperative Work (CSCW) 2004 conference that tested the effects of ingroup and outgroup bias on mixed groups of collocated and remote team members. Suspecting that the natural tendency would be towards greater collaboration among collocated members than among collocated members and remote members, they presented the following hypotheses: 1) Individuals working in the same location will interact more with each other, forming an in-group; 2) In response, those individuals that are isolated will create a separate in-group; and 3) Individuals working in the same location will outperform those who are isolated because they can better coordinate and because they belong to the in-group.

The methodology used by Bos, et al (2004) was the Shape Factory simulation environment, which is an experimental task used to study patterns of collaboration among groups in a number of configurations (for example, face to face instead of communicating via computer) and geographical

41

settings (working together in one location or remotely). The simulation involves ten players using an online game trying to fill orders for their own particular shape-color combination, such as "Blue Square, Purple Circle." The orders for each player in each round contained a total of eight shapes, so players had to buy shapes from each other. They also had to sell their own unique shapes to other players. To maximize earnings they would sell specialized shapes to other players and assemble the shapes they had purchased into specific orders. Each player's performance in the study was measured by the game score from filling orders and selling shapes, along with how many shapes each had bought and sold. Thirteen 20-minute sessions were conducted, with teams consisting of 5 members collocated in the same room and 5 members each isolated in different rooms, but connected with the rest of the group through the game platform (Bos, et al, 2004).

The results of the study supported the first hypothesis, as those team members working in the same location demonstrated a strong tendency to work with each other instead of with the remote participants. The second hypothesis was also confirmed, although the remote participants did not seem to be aware of the formation of their own in-group; rather, the formation of the group seemed to come about as an unconscious response to being ignored by the collocated members. Surprisingly, though, the third hypothesis was disproven, because average scores of collocated players and remote group members did not differ (Bos, et al, 2004).

The authors of the study identified a number of potential weaknesses in their methodology. Some criticism exists of the Shape Factory environment because it is viewed as not accurately reflecting the levels of competition and collaboration involved in most teamwork. The simulated work environment of the remote participants was criticized as not being entirely realistic because most remote group members would have a wider choice of means of communication with the collocated group and other remote members than simple text messaging (Bos, et al, 2004). However, the author of this project shares the opinion of the researchers that these criticisms do not significantly weaken the conclusions of the study; in fact, if anything, better communication would only serve to enhance the remote participants' performance instead of lowering it.

An interesting area for future study would be to look for ways to integrate remote members into the collocators' ingroup. Given that the performance of remote members does not seem to be diminished by not being physically present with other members (Bos, et al, 2004), it seems logical that increasing the level of communication of the remote members through increased video conferencing and the use of other technology might cause remote members to actually outperform collocated members.

Context

Anthropologist Edward Hall produced seminal work on intercultural communication and is credited with the popularization of the idea of classifying cultures by level of context (high or low). According to Hall (1976, 1981, p. 39), people in high context cultures tend to be deeply involved with each other; information is widely shared and simple messages with deep meanings flow freely. He observes that high context cultures risk being overwhelmed by mechanical systems and losing their integrity – an observation that seems less likely to be completely accurate in today's technology-infused society than it would have been at the time of Hall's writing, yet nevertheless may hold true in a broader sense. In low context cultures, on the other hand, people are marked by high levels of individualization with relatively low levels of involvement with other people. Messages must be much more detailed in low context cultures, because less of the meaning of the communication can be derived from the environment. These cultures, observes Hall, seem to be able to absorb and use man-made mechanical extensions and still preserve their integrity. China reflects a high-context culture, while America – and even more extremely, Germany, Switzerland and Scandinavia – are lower-context cultures (Hall, 1976, 1981, p. 91).

Hall points out that, in linguistics, simple knowledge of a linguistic code is not sufficient for understanding (1976, 1981, p. 86). He observes that context has much to do with conveying the meaning of the linguistic code, and that, if taken out of context, this code is incomplete because it does not carry the full message. Hall underscores the critical nature of context by pointing out that the level of context has everything to do with determining the nature of the communication, and that all subsequent behavior is built on it (Hall, 1976, 1981, p. 92). He also asserts that effective communication requires investing a certain amount of time in contexting the other party to the conversation so that the information making up the explicit portions of the message is neither inadequate nor excessive (Hall, 1976, 1981, pp. 92-93). This is consistent with research by Scribner & Cole (1978) on the Vai of western Africa, where letters written among Vai people frequently began with an explanation to the reader that he or she should expect to receive information via the written word in the letter, thus contextualizing the communication for the otherwise largely unschooled reader. Furthermore, Hall (1976, 1981, p. 93) observes that modern management methods are less successful than they should be because they frequently fail to take into account what people already know as they attempt to make everything explicit (low context).

The idea of context connects to the concept of ingroup and outgroup bias because there is a greater distinction made between insiders and outsiders in high context cultures (Hall, 1976, 1981, p. 112). Hall also points out that individuals from high context cultures are less likely to communicate their needs or frustrations directly and will "talk around" the subject because they expect the hearer to understand what is bothering them. This is because stating the conclusion for the listener is tantamount to an insult and a violation of his or her individuality. This tendency, of course, can be quite frustrating to listeners from low context societies such as the United States, who often become irritated at speakers from other cultures for "beating around the bush."

One observation by Hall (1976, 1981, p. 127) is particularly relevant to the subject of this paper. He asserts that low context individuals who attempt to interact with high context cultures can expect trouble if they do not pay close attention to planning for contingencies. This realization could be crucial to improving communications between the home office of Organization A in the United States and the field.

Trompenaars & Hampden-Turner (1998, p. 83) approach the idea of high and low context cultures from a slightly different angle, referring to them as "specific" or "diffuse" cultures. People from specific cultures interact with other people in compartmentalized areas of life and levels of personality, while people from diffuse cultures engage others in many different areas of life and levels of personality simultaneously. Rather than maintaining a constant level of authority over an employee in all instances, a manager in a specific culture may defer to an employee's greater expertise in a social engagement such as a game of golf, thus compartmentalizing his influence in the employee's life and making each encounter a specific case where influence is judged by the context of the encounter. However, in diffuse cultures, status remains fixed at all levels of interaction, be they personal or business.

This approach thinks of life as being divided into public and private spaces. In diffuse cultures, public spaces are small and private spaces are harder to enter; but once an individual is admitted to someone's private space, they are granted broad access to almost all areas of that private space. In contrast, in specific or low context cultures, the public spaces are broad and compartmentalized into many areas, while private spaces are difficult to access. An individual's colleagues may feel free to call on him or her at work, but feel unwelcome to "intrude" in the individual's private life (Trompenaars & Hampden-Turner, 1998, pp. 84-85).

Potential arises for conflict between specific and diffuse cultures in the area of criticism. In specific cultures, it is possible to criticize an individual's idea without criticizing the person. However, in a diffuse culture, the individual's ideas are inextricably interwoven with his or her personality, and criticism of one's ideas constitutes personal criticism (Trompenaars & Hampden-Turner, 1998, p. 87). This, too, could prove to be an invaluable insight for communicators at Organization A.

For a person from a specific culture to establish a productive business relationship with an individual from a diffuse culture can be a time-consuming project. Trompenaars & Hampden-Turner (1998, p. 89) point out that some cultures refuse to do business in a compartmentalized space known as "commerce" or "work," insisting instead on first getting to know their business counterpart as a person and learning about where he or she went to school, his or her political views, and personal interests such as hobbies. While specific cultures prefer to enter business negotiations with few preliminaries, get to the heart of the matter and move on, many businesspeople from diffuse cultures spend much more time in the negotiating process in pleasantries and socializing. Once this all-important hurdle has been crossed and personal rapport has been established, the actual matter of business may take relatively little time.

Trompenaars & Hampden-Turner (1998, p. 92) refer to low context and high context cultures as specific and diffuse cultures, respectively. They explain that context has to do with how much information a person must have in order to communicate effectively, the unspoken assumption of common knowledge between conversants, and the level of reference to tacit common ground. They further observe that people in high context cultures believe it is necessary to brief strangers before proper discussion of business can take place, while low context cultures believe each participant, stranger or not, should take part in making the rules, and that a minimum of structure is desirable initially. Finally, they assert that specific or low context cultures tend to look at objects, specifics and things before considering how these are related, while diffuse or high context cultures tend to look at relationships and connections before considering all the separate pieces, with the two contexts forming a circular relationship.

Additionally, Trompenaars & Hampden-Turner (1998, pp. 92-93) identify how high context and low context cultures differ in management philosophy. Managers in low context cultures favor MBO (management by objectives) and pay-for-performance as motivators. This emphasizes these cultures' specific orientation, focusing on the objective and establishing improvement in performance as a means of achieving better and more productive relationships between managers and employees. However, high context cultures focus more on the relationship between subordinates and superiors as the originator of better performance – two diametrically opposed perspectives on the same situation. These deep-seated differences in perspective and philosophy can have a strong bearing on the effectiveness of intercultural communication.

Face

Storti (1994, p. 67) describes face as " the image one presents to the world, including one's reputation," observing that face is "closely linked to the notion of self-esteem or self-worth...and if at all possible one does not want to lose one's face, especially in public." Ho, Fu & Ng (2004) affirm that loss of face causes social damage, reveals a person's actions to public scrutiny and negative judgment, and undermines the individual's moral or social standing. Trompenaars & Hampden-Turner (1998, p. 88) explain that loss of face occurs when something is made public which people perceive as being private. Gudykunst (2005, p. 18) cites the assertion by Cupach & Imahori (1993) that being able to avoid loss of face in interactions reflects on a person's competence in interpersonal communication. Building on the work of Reeder (1987), McFarlin & Sweeney (2006, p. 174) observe that the need for face (the regard of others) may be the single most important concept to be aware of in many Asian cultures, and that, since many Asian cultures are interdependent, they also try to save face for others.

McFarlin & Sweeney (2006, p. 174) point out that, in some cultures, to not know is to lose face. Therefore, an individual may provide information that is inaccurate rather than not provide information at all. Furthermore, because the affording of face is mutual, individuals in these cultures might proceed according to someone's instructions even knowing that the outcome would be undesirable rather than cause the other party to lose face by pointing out that their instructions were flawed. In discussing Japanese culture, McFarlin & Sweeney (2006, p. 200) observe that the Japanese tend to avoid explicitly saying no to the other party so that both sides retain face, relying instead on a variety of indirect ways of saying no.

Citing Cohen (1997), Rosenberg (2004) states that preserving face and maintaining group harmony is core to high context communication, and that said communication should be preceded by careful consideration of each word and should include an abundance of expressions of respect and courtesy, because rebuffing someone could result in loss of face. Trompenaars & Hampden-Turner (1998, p. 88) explain that people in diffuse or high context cultures often take longer to get to the point in their communications precisely because of the danger of causing loss of face. Communicators must avoid direct confrontation because it is impossible for participants not to take things personally.

Uncertainty Avoidance

Hofstede's Uncertainty Avoidance Index addresses how much uncertainty and ambiguity a society will tolerate, or the extent to which it conditions its members to experience comfort or discomfort in unstructured situations. Cultures that avoid uncertainty attempt to avoid unstructured situations. They also hold to the belief that there is one absolute truth, and that they have it. People in these cultures tend to be more emotional. On the other hand, cultures that accept uncertainty tend to be more tolerant of differing opinions, have fewer rules and are more relativist in areas of philosophy and politics, and their people tend to be more phlegmatic, more contemplative and less communicative of emotions. Cultures that are high context tend to be uncertainty avoidant, while cultures that are low context have a greater tolerance for uncertainty (Hofstede, 2009).

Tuleja & O'Rourke (2009, p. 73) observe that low uncertainty-avoidance cultures deal with uncertainty by building coping mechanisms through technology, law and religion. High uncertainty-avoidance cultures, however, attempt to prevent unstructured situations by maximizing predictability through establishing rules and strict codes of behavior, apparently embracing the motto that "what is different is dangerous."

Dealing with uncertainty and change can also affect the way cultures communicate. High uncertainty-avoiding cultures are more oriented toward the ingroup and more cautious about getting to know people outside it. This is logical, because high uncertainty-avoiding cultures are closely correlated with communitarian or collectivist cultures, where emphasis is placed on the importance of establishing relationships based upon connection within the greater community, paying special attention to status and family origin. Business characteristics of these cultures may include a lengthier time required to integrate new employees into long-standing workgroups, more dependency on the authority and direction provided by leaders, less tolerance of risk, and more preoccupation with consensus and harmony for the good of the greater group than what would be found in less uncertainty-avoidant cultures (Tuleja & O'Rourke, 2009, p. 75).

Masculinity/Femininity

Another of Hofstede's (2009) cultural dimensions is masculinity versus femininity, or how roles are distributed between the genders. He cites research indicating that women's values are far more consistent among societies than are those of men, and that men's values from country to country may range from highly competitive and assertive (as well as differing strongly from women's values) to modest, caring and relating closely to women's values. Culture in the United States is generally rated as highly masculine, while many high-context cultures tend to be more feminine. However, research by Sørnes, Stephens, Sætre, & Browning (2004) reveals that American culture seems to be trending more feminine in recent years, which may correlate to Americans' use of communications technology in an increasingly feminine fashion (for example, moving away from using information technology primarily as a business tool and toward social media as a means of building, extending and maintaining relationships). Of interest also is the fact that region and common language do not seem to be determining factors in nations' levels of cultural masculinity; for example, MAS (masculinity) scores vary widely in Latin America, from 69 in Mexico to 28 in Chile, with Ecuador at (63) and Colombia at (64) – all of these being countries in which Organization A works – coming in stronger in cultural masculinity than the United States at 62 ("World map," 2011).

Harmony

Assertiveness and interpersonal harmony are cultural dimensions that are inextricably intertwined. Samovar, Porter & McDaniel (2009, p. 291) argue that while some cultures such as America and Germany see assertiveness as an asset, other cultures view it as "threatening and detrimental to genial interpersonal relationships." Of particular interest to this study because of Organization A's presence in the Philippines, Samovar, et al (2009, p. 291) observe that the Filipino culture places particular value on interpersonal harmony, explaining that the Filipino concept of harmony relates to a "very fragile sense of personal worth and self-respect." They add that Filipinos are especially vulnerable to negative remarks that might affect their standing in society (making the ideas of harmony and face closely related), and that Filipinos rarely criticize or confront others, using extreme politeness when criticism or confrontations are unavoidable. Bluntness and frankness are viewed as uncivilized traits.

This outlook is diametrically opposed to American culture, whose roots are deeply entrenched in individualism, with attributes of competitiveness, free speech and nonconformity. The combination of these elements greatly increases the likelihood of people engaging in assertive behavior (Samovar, et al, 2009, p. 291). On the other hand, Japanese often are so averse to confrontation that they refuse to say "no," resorting instead to more evasive responses, while the Mexican culture values harmony so much that the concept of truth may become situational – so much so that "in order to sustain positive relations or make the other person feel better, Mexicans may slightly alter the facts or withhold important negative information" (Samovar, et al, 2009, p. 291). Meanwhile, Frith (1994) echoes Kincaid's (1987) assertion that keeping social harmony is paramount to communication within most Asian cultures.

Time

Perhaps no cultural dimension can be as perplexing to those of different cultures as the way other cultures perceive time. Hall (1983, pp. 42-43) makes the provocative observation that [Anglo Americans] "tend to think that because nothing overt is happening, nothing is going on." He then adds that with many cultures there are long periods during which people are making up their minds or waiting for consensus to be achieved, concluding that "we would do well to pay more attention to these things."

Hall (1983, p. 46) divides time into two major perspectives: polychronic and monochronic. In polychronic time, people do many things at once, while in monochronic time people tend to be more linear (Hall, 1983, p. 45). Cultures that are high context lean toward polychronicity, while those that are low context tend to be more monochronic.

Typical of polychronic cultures are scenes common throughout Latin America and other areas of the world where individuals vie for the attention of clerks in stores or marketplaces with no apparent order or queuing process to indicate who should be served next. Hall (1983, p. 47) observes that North Americans can frequently be psychologically stressed by such surroundings. He also remarks on the stress North Americans experience when faced with the way polychronic people handle appointments, pointing out that time in polychronic cultures simply does not bear the same meaning as it does in the United States, a monochronic culture. Where events in the lives of North Americans tend to be rigidly governed by time and schedules, matters in a polychronic culture appear to be constantly in flux, where nothing is concrete (especially as regards the future) and important plans are subject to change up until the very last moment.

Hall (1983, p. 48) contrasts this perspective with that of monochronic cultures, where time is deeply ingrained in the psyche of the culture to the point that its overarching influence, including on interpersonal relationships, is often unconsciously overlooked. He explains that by scheduling we are able to compartmentalize, allowing us to concentrate on one thing at a time; however, this concentration comes at the expense of context. Monochronic time is so completely ingrained into Western culture that it is perceived as the only way of organizing life that is natural and logical, yet this type of time is neither native to man's biological rhythms nor existential in nature (Hall, 1983, pp. 48-49). Hall further observes that monochronic time often limits people's primary involvement with others due to the rigors and limitations of scheduling.

In contrast, people from polychronic cultures interact with several people at one time and are continually involved with each other, making tight scheduling difficult if not impossible (Hall, 1983, p. 49). They are so deeply immersed in each others' business that they feel a compulsion to stay in touch, having a truly extraordinary knowledge of each other. Their involvement in people is the core of their existence, which results in a proliferation of small bureaucracies really not set up to handle the needs of outsiders, meaning one must be an insider or have a well-situated friend to make something happen (Hall, 1983, p. 50).

A very interesting aspect of the polychronic time orientation is that supervisors in polychronic societies may provide a subordinate with a very detailed list of activities to be completed in order to satisfactorily discharge his or her responsibilities, but they would never presume to schedule the execution of those activities, because "for an employer to schedule a subordinate's work for him would be considered a tyrannical violation of his individuality – an invasion of the self" (Hall, 1983, p. 50). This contrasts with monochronic cultures' tendency to schedule the activity and leave the analysis of the activities of the job to the individual. Further, polychronic cultures remind the subordinate that his or her job is part of a larger system, whereas people in monochronic cultures are less likely to see their activities in context or as part of the larger whole; while they are aware of the organization, it is less likely for monochronic people to connect their jobs directly to the goals of the organization (Hall, 1983, pp. 50-51).

In his analysis, Hall (1983) acknowledges that both time orientations – monochronic and polychronic – have inherent weaknesses. He points out that polychronic organizations are limited in size, depend on having gifted people at the top and are slow and cumbersome when dealing with anything new or different, creating the risk of bureaucratic disaster. On the other hand, organizations that are monochronic often overlook the humanity of their members (Hall, 1983, pp. 51-52). Polychronic cultures are, by nature, people-oriented; in these cultures, one cannot cut people off because of a schedule. They must be heard out because they are valued. In contrast, monochronic cultures are oriented to tasks, schedules and procedures, thus relegating humanity and employee morale to a place of lesser prominence (Hall, 1983, pp. 53-54).

Hall (1983, pp. 53-55) identifies other potential sources of tension between people from polychronic and monochronic cultures. In polychronic, people-oriented cultures, family takes precedence over all else, with friends coming in a close second. Polychronic people will generally try to fit unscheduled favors to family or friends into scheduled events, which can cause consternation to the monochronic businessperson or customer. Should the accommodation fail to be made, however, there may be endless repercussions from the "slighted" friends or family members. Additionally, Hall (1983, p. 55) points out that the degree of accommodation and who is pushed aside to make it is in itself a communication; the more important the customer or business that is postponed or disrupted to grant the favor, the more reassured the favored family member or friend will feel. Therefore, the way to ensure the message that one is accepted or loved in a polychronic culture is, according to Hall, to call up at the last minute and expect everyone to rearrange everything to accommodate the change, with a failure to do this being perceived as a clear signal that the other party simply does not care enough. To a monochronic person caught in this kind of pattern, this preferential treatment of family and friends can be an insurmountable obstacle. In instances like these where patterns of culture seem destined to collide, Hall (1983, p. 55) asserts that the point of conflict must be identified before there can be any hope of resolution. What happens is one side or the other literally gives up, and a customer or relationship is lost.

Trompenaars and Hampden-Turner (1998, p. 123) add depth to the concept of time and culture by pointing out that the way we perceive time has practical effects. They present two views of time: synchronic and sequential. The synchronic view of time blends past, present and future in such a way that future projections and past memories combine to influence present action, while the sequential view sees life as a string of passing events.

Trompenaars and Hampden-Turner (1998, p. 124) refer to the assertion of Kluckhohn & Strodtbeck (1960) that there are three types of culture: present-oriented, past-oriented and future oriented. Cultures that are oriented to the present are relatively unchanging and have few traditions, with little regard for the future; cultures that are past-oriented strive mainly to maintain and restore traditions, while cultures that are future-oriented envision a preferred future and set out to realize it. Trompenaars and Hampden-Turner observe that people from future-oriented cultures are those who generally experience economic or social development. Additionally, they posit that attraction to past, present or future orientations may vary by individual and by culture.

In further examining the concept of time in light of culture, Trompenaars and Hampden-Turner (1998, p. 126) extract two images: that of time as a series of regularly-spaced sequential events passing, and that of time as cyclical and repetitive, blending the past, the present and the future by their shared characteristics of seasons and rhythms. Viewing time as sequential, or following a straight line from Point A to Point B with minimum effort and maximum effect, is termed "efficiency;" however, this line of thinking may be flawed if it fails to recognize that following straight lines may not always be the best way of doing things because it ignores the effectiveness of shared activities and cross-connections.

However, the synchronic or polychronic method requires tracking various activities in parallel, which presents a challenge to cultures that are unused to doing so (Trompenaars & Hampden-Turner, 1998, p. 127). With this method there is a final and established goal, but one arrives at it through the use of numerous, possibly interchangeable stepping stones. This is fundamentally different from the linearity of the sequential or monochronic method, which follows a "crucial path" with predetermined milestones. Monochronic people are averse to having their schedules disrupted by unanticipated events, a characteristic that might present a vulnerability to negotiators from a synchronic culture (Hall & Hall, 1990, p. 20).

Trompenaars and Hampden-Turner (1998, p. 127) observe that synchronic or polychronic styles can seem extraordinary to people from cultures with a different time orientation. The ability of polychronic individuals to effectively multitask may be interpreted by monochronic people as a slight, leaving them feeling as though they are not being paid proper attention. Equally puzzling to the monochronic person is the polychronic individual's apparent lack of preoccupation with punctuality, and vice versa: polychronic individuals may be fascinated with monochronic people's seeming obsession with schedules and punctuality. This results from a fundamental difference in philosophies toward time: to the sequential or monochronic person, time is a commodity to be used up, and lateness bears a cost because "time is money;" to the polychronic or synchronous person, however, several cultural values vie with punctuality for preeminence, including the need to give time to people with whom one has a relationship, which could result in temporary delaying of appointments or late starts for meetings (Trompenaars & Hampden-Turner, 1998, p. 128). This makes sense given the fact that polychronic societies tend to be high context and collectivist, placing great value on people and relationships.

Interestingly, polychronicity may actually allow improved productivity in the workplace. Kaufman-Scarborough & Lindquist (1999) refer to research by Bluedorn and Denhardt (1988), Feldman and Hornik (1981), and Lane, Kaufman, and Lindquist (1989) to establish that individuals can perform multiple activities in a specified period of time and that using time polychronically may lead to an output that exceeds that of a monochronic time use (Kaufman, Lane and Lindquist, 1991). This being the case, global or multinational organizations based in monochronic societies would do well to carefully consider the potential for increased productivity in their polychronic locations rather than be dismissive of polychronic work styles because they do not conform to the monochronic ideas that are endemic to many management theories.

One difference between monochronic and polychronic perspectives that we have already touched on briefly and that can have a significant impact on intercultural business relationships is how schedules and appointments are perceived. In monochronic cultures, schedules tend to be inflexible, taking priority above everything else and being treated as almost sacred (Hall & Hall, 1990, p. 13), whereas in polychronic cultures there is greater emphasis on human interaction than on timetables or schedules (Hall & Hall, 1990, p. 14). While in monochronic cultures to keep someone waiting for a business appointment is regarded as an insult, this is not generally true in polychronic cultures, where people tend to do many things at one time and are expected to accommodate friends, family and close business associates before all others (Hall & Hall, 1990, pp. 21-22).

Hall & Hall (1990, p. 15) summarize important stereotypical differences between people of monochronic cultures (monochronics) and polychronic cultures (polychronics). They argue that people from monochronic cultures generally:

- Do one thing at a time, while polychronics do many things at once
- Concentrate on the job, while polychronics are highly distractible and subject to interruptions
- Take time commitments such as deadlines and schedules seriously, while polychronics consider time commitments an objective to be achieved if possible
- Are low-context and need information, while polychronics are high context and already have information
- Are committed to the job, while polychronics are committed to people and human relationships
- Adhere religiously to plans, while polychronics change plans often and easily
- Are concerned about not disturbing others and follow rules of privacy and consideration, while polychronics are more concerned with those who are closely related, such as family, friends and close business associates, than with privacy
- Show great respect for private property, seldom borrowing or lending, while polychronics borrow and lend often and easily

- Emphasize promptness, while polychronics base promptness on the relationship, and
- Are accustomed to short-term relationships, while polychronics have a strong tendency to build lifetime relationships.

Power Distance

The way people perceive power in different cultures can be an important factor in intercultural business communication. Hofstede (2009) describes power distance as the willingness of organizations or institutions to concede or expect that power is not distributed equally. He further observes that power distance speaks of inequality as defined from below, and argues that it is simply a fact that power and inequality exist in any society, with some being more unequal than others.

Ahmed, Mouratidis & Preston (2009) relied on the research of Hall (1976) and Wurtz (2005) to conclude that Western/Northern European cultures tend to be low power distance, while Mediterranean, Asian and Latin American cultures lean toward high power distance. Francesco & Chen (2000) of Hong Kong Baptist University studied how power distance affects the influence of participation on the variables of organizational commitment, job satisfaction, intention to stay, and performance, indicating that participation and each of the aforementioned variables are positively correlated proportionate to how each respondent was oriented toward power distance. In respondents with low orientation to power distance, the positive relationship was observed; however, virtually no relationship existed for those oriented to high power distance. This suggests that attitude and behavior of people with low power distance orientation can be far more easily affected by participation than is likely for those otherwise oriented.

The Impact of Cultural Variability on Communication

Gudykunst (1997) relies on existing data from a variety of researchers to study the effects of cultural variability on communication. Although the research materials did not originate with him, Gudykunst applied clearly-defined methodological rules as he selected the research on which he would base his analysis: the authors had to clearly demonstrate why their theory expected communication to vary by culture, and their research had to be grounded in accepted cross-cultural procedures; furthermore, he sought to include studies reflecting a wide cross-section of contexts and research procedures.

In his article, Gudykunst (1997) differentiates between emic approaches (which study behavior from within a cultural system) and etic approaches (which study behavior from outside a cultural system), explaining that most anthropological research on culture is emic, while research that is more sociological or psychological is etic. He examines the effects of several etic cultural aspects on communication: individualism-collectivism (Chinese Culture Connection, 1987; Hofstede, 1980; Ito, 1989; Kluckhohn & Strodtbeck, 1961; Triandis, 1995), uncertainty avoidance (Hofstede, 1979, 1980, 1991), power distance (Hofstede & Bond, 1984), and masculinity-femininity (Hofstede, 1980; Gudykunst & Nishida, 1983; Gudykunst, Yang & Nishida, 1985; Nishida, 1986; Wheeler, 1988). Gudykunst concludes that, while certain aspects of cultural variability are stronger in different cultures, it is impossible to fully understand similarities and differences in communications among cultures using a single cultural variability aspect; rather, this requires different combinations of variability aspects.

Martin, Hammer & Bradford (1994) carried out a study to attempt to measure the impact of certain aspects of cultural variability (in particular, collectivism and individualism) on people's expectations regarding competent communication behavior, using the earlier work of two of the researchers (Martin & Hammer, 1989) and advanced based on three assumptions: (1) people's expectations for what constitutes competent communication behavior can be identified, (2) the assessment of the competence of behaviors rests on these expectations, and (3) both situational and individual variables may affect these expectations. The two groups chosen for comparison were White (Anglo) Americans of European descent and Hispanic Americans. Based on prior research (Bellah, et al., 1985; Hofstede, 1980, 1984, 1991; Kluckhohn & Strodtbeck, 1961; Condon, 1985; Cangotena, 1994; Marin & Marin, 1991; Marin & Triandis, 1985; Triandis, Marin, Lisansky, & Betancourt, 1984), White Americans were assumed to be culturally individualistic while Hispanic Americans were assumed to be more collectivist.

The research seems to proceed on the hypothesis that people with common ethnic socialization patters also share similarities in expectations for competent communication behavior, but the same may not be true for people who experience alternate ethnic socialization patterns. Respondents included 225 Hispanic-Americans and 209 White non-Hispanic respondents from two large universities in the Southwestern United States. The respondents were subjected to a chi-square statistical comparison, but no significant differences were found between the groups when it came to gender, age or previous international experience. Additionally, both Hispanic and non-Hispanic respondents to the study appear to have come from similar socioeconomic backgrounds (Martin, et al, 1994). Respondents were given a questionnaire to rate the importance of communication behaviors in creating impressions of competence in initial interaction cultural (intercultural vs. intracultural) contexts and in situational (social vs. task) contexts.

Results were supportive of the hypothesis. One trend that seemed to surface was that context may influence Hispanic and non-Hispanic judgments differently for some behaviors; in other words, behavioral expectations may differ depending on whether one is operating within or outside of one's own cultural group.

Tran & Skitmore (2002) conducted a study on the impact of culture on national management. The survey was conducted among 36 construction managers in Singapore, a location chosen for its high context/low individuality orientation and the fluency of its residents in the English language (to avoid the possibility of skewing results because of errors in translation of the survey questionnaire). Among the factors considered in the survey was the impact of uncertainty avoidance on communication.

The study by Tran & Skitmore (2002) found a positive correlation between a national culture of relatively low uncertainty avoidance and the importance placed on communicating with those outside the organization, implying that the tendency of these cultures to encourage personal initiative and individual responsibility for actions may be a factor. The study also indicated that low uncertainty-avoidance cultures are built on more trusting relationships and therefore require less formal means of business communication, while high uncertainty-avoidance cultures tend to rely on more formal means of communication. This could explain why, at Organization A, an informal memo from the home office in the United States might be perceived at the international agencies as carrying less weight than an officially-worded request, although to the low context, low uncertainty-avoidance writer in America it may simply have been perceived as a less officious but equally binding communication.

When combined with the effects of the automatic formation of a separate ingroup among remote members of a work team per the findings of Bos, et al (2004), confusion generated among high-context, high uncertainty avoidance readers (which describes most of Organization A's communications coordinators) by receipt of a low-context, informal message from the home office (such as might typically come in the form of an email) could easily ensue; due to communication among ingroup members in the field, this confusion could be quickly generalized to most or all field agencies without the sender of the message at the home office becoming aware of the uneasiness or consternation in the field until later. This is a very real consideration in its relevance to the study at hand.

Olk (2009) sheds light on a different aspect of cultural variability and its impact on communication: the degree of familiarity the communicator has with cultural references in both the source and target languages. His research involved a group of 19 British individuals who were studying German and who were asked to translate an English-language article from a well-known publication into German and to journal their thought processes as they did so. The methodology for selection of the cultural references involved performing a search of the Guardian's archives (www.guardians.com.uk) to ensure the references occurred with enough frequency to qualify as "common." The students were provided numerous bilingual dictionaries to ensure their choices would be procedural and not the result of a lack of knowledge of appropriate terminology.

Problems the students encountered ranged from unfamiliarity with widely-understood cultural references in their own language to the issue of trying to determine the understandability of these cultural references in the target language and the difficulty of finding target-language terms that adequately explained the references. A large percentage had difficulty distinguishing culturally-based differences in the meanings of common terms; for example, 68% of participants seemed unaware of differences between the German term "Berufe" and "the professions" (as relates to the English "old professions) that were specific to culture, while 74% did not immediately know the standard translation for "Victorian" in German, illustrating a lack of knowledge of target-language terminology related to cultural references.

Olk's (2009) study is not unassailable. The fact that it was carried out with such a small group (19 participants) renders it statistically insignificant and highly vulnerable to bias. Nevertheless, its implications are highly germane to the study at hand; when issuing assignments from the central office in the United States, Organization A personnel tend to employ a casual style of writing that is heavily laced with slang and colloquialisms, which, although intended to put the reader at ease, can be extremely difficult for recipients who are not native to the English language or North American culture to comprehend. Adler (1997) addresses this tendency by Americans who seek to develop closer relationships to use a casual communication style; while the intent of the U.S.-based staff is to build trust and put the reader at ease, the effect may well be the opposite: unfamiliarity with casual cultural references may confuse the non-U.S. reader and heighten his or her sense of anxiety.

A study by Seo, Miller, Schmidt and Sowa (2008) examines how cultural variability affects online communications. In light of research by Hofstede (1986, 1997), Hall & Hall (1989) and Gudykunst et al (1988) that points to differences in communication based on cultural factors such as context, individualism-collectivism and time orientation (long-term versus short-term), Seo and her colleagues examined the online communication styles of two groups of students: one from Hong Kong and one from America.

The methodology of the study by Seo, et al (2008), involved 83 undergraduate students in the U.S. and 59 students in Hong Kong (H.K.) enrolled in the same course either on campus or through the university's distance learning program. The students from each culture were grouped separately and required to participate in online threaded discussions, which for the first week consisted of personal introductions. The next three weeks' postings were a discussion on environmental concerns, and the following three weeks' discussions were devoted to health and medical concerns. The students took a survey during the final week to assess their online discussions. Seo, et al (2008) performed a comparison of number of pages visited, number of posts read, and number of messages submitted between the two groups. This was followed by an analysis of the content of the students' responses to messages, narrowing the responses down to three types: those that agreed, those that disagreed and those that offered an alternative.

The results of the study were strongly confirmatory of the known communication differences between individualist and collectivist cultures. Seo, et al (2008) reported that a lower percentage of Hong Kong students than U.S. students disagreed, with students from Hong Kong disagreeing 1.23% of the time versus 1.76% for U.S. students. Additionally, students from Hong Kong (collectivist) tended to disagree indirectly, while students from the U.S. (individualist) disagreed in a more straightforward manner. This supports the observation by Wei, Yuen and Zhu (2001), based on existing research (Ohbuchi et al., 1999; Morris et al., 1998; Ohbuchi & Takahashi, 1994; Trubisky et al., 1991), that collectivism gravitates toward communication that is indirect and passive and toward styles of conflict management that avoid or oblige, while individualism tends toward forms of expression that are more direct and active. Examples of these are the competing and dominating styles of conflict management. In some countries, such as Japan, this trait of conflict avoidance can manifest itself in an unwillingness to say "no," which can prove misleading to individuals unfamiliar with the culture (Storti, 1994).

This may prove to have a direct bearing on some of the difficulties at Organization A with communications coordinators (CCs) failing to meet deadlines. Aside from the fact that almost all the CCs come from polychronic cultures, most also come from collectivist (and, consequently, conflict-avoidant) cultures. Therefore, even if their schedules clearly will not accommodate a request by a specific deadline, it may be difficult for them to express that clearly enough for the American manager to understand.

Yuan (2009) did a study on the effectiveness of communication between American and Chinese employees of multinational organizations in China using information from Hofstede (1980, 2001) Hall (1989), Gudykunst and Ting-Toomey (1988), Gudykunst (2002), and others. Yuan's hypothesis is that multinational organizations can improve the intercultural effectiveness of their employees by incorporating the findings of the study into their internal training programs.

The basic platform of Yuan's (2009) study draws on Hofstede's (1980) national cultural dimensions, with a primary focus on the dimensions of individualism-collectivism and power distance, as well as personal interviews with 42 employees of

28 multinational organizations. The respondents included 20 non-Chinese Americans, 19 Chinese, and 3 Chinese Americans. All study-related communications were conducted in English. All respondents were employees of 28 multinationals that operated in China and represented industries such as telecommunications, accounting, advertising, public relations, agriculture, cosmetics, manufacturing, information technology, and legal services.

The questions Yuan (2009) researched were 1) How do American and Chinese employees think about the effectiveness of communication between them, and 2) What kinds of barriers do American and Chinese employees encounter during their interaction? Yuan used firsthand, face-to-face interviews using semi-structured interview protocol to collect the data, and then transcribed all audio interviews verbatim and translated Chinese responses to English for analysis using a constant comparative method identify categories and thematic patterns.

According to Yuan's (2009) study, only roughly a third of the respondents considered themselves to be effective in intercultural communication. Others rated themselves as "ok," "somewhat effective," or "depending on circumstances." Yuan concludes that these self-ratings show participants applied different criteria to evaluate their effectiveness in communication, such as the quality of work relationships, their ability to complete tasks, or their success in getting points across. Some regarded task completion as the goal of intercultural communication, while others valued clarity and accuracy above other criteria. Most respondents agreed that intercultural communication is not as smooth and effective as communication within one's own culture, although some expressed they felt their intercultural communication became more effective over time. However, others expressed that underlying cultural differences would always present an obstacle to effective intercultural communications. In fact, one of the conclusions of the study is that all of the respondents reported encountering communication barriers of one sort or another, to include differences in thought patterns, variations in communication style, a shortage of shared knowledge and organizational structures that lacked efficiency.

Overall, Yuan's (2009) study seems to support previous research, especially as relates Hofstede's (1980) cultural dimensions. The methodology seems appropriate to the research, and the findings are consistent with the idea that culture is a major component in effective business communication. Possible limitations of the study include the fact that it was conducted entirely within the context of multinational organizations, which implies that Chinese participants may have become somewhat Westernized because of their environment, and that all respondents were unknown to Yuan prior to participating in the study, which could affect their willingness to participate candidly. However, it is doubtful these factors would be significant enough to skew the study's results.

Yuan (2009) uses the findings of the study to suggest a number of areas for future investigation:

1. Macro-level examination of communication within multinational organizations instead of the interpersonal level used for the existing study.

2. Interviews of matched pairs of intercultural respondents to evaluate their perceptions of and reactions to an identical situation in an organizational setting.

3. Perform a longitudinal study of a multinational organization spanning a number of years in order to yield a more accurate analysis of the effects of cultural assimilation.

4. Conduct a similar study in different contexts to evaluate the effects of the external environment on intercultural communication in the workplace.

An additional area of future study that could serve as an outgrowth of Yuan's (2009) research might include a comparison of respondents' perceptions based on virtual or remote intercultural communication versus face-to-face interaction, in order to determine the importance of visual cues from context in the ability to correctly decode communication.

Face-Based Issues in Intercultural Conflict

Chang (2011) studied the effects of issues of negative and positive face on intercultural communications and conflict, hypothesizing that face-based goal issues, if not properly managed, can lead to unresolved conflicts. Citing the work of Ting-Toomey (2005) and others, Chang points out that identity-based conflicts arise when there is a discrepancy between how people perceive they should be treated and how they actually are treated. Positive face needs are defined as people's needs to be respected, honored, included, approved, liked, and considered competent and trustworthy, while negative face deals with their need for privacy, independence, autonomy, freedom, and the right to make their own decisions.

Chang's (2011) research is based on a series of actual emails exchanged between a visiting American professor and the International Office of a university in China. The emails demonstrate escalating tensions on both sides as the professor complains of contractual failure to provide him adequate living quarters and reimbursement for certain expenses. Because the professor and the Chinese university representative fail to recognize each other's face needs from the beginning, each continues to attempt to defend their sense of identity while repeatedly offending the other.

In the research, Chang (2011) identifies several communication patterns that contributed to the conflict. These include:

1) Conflict-driven interactions (the subjects initiated communication with each other only to resolve problems or issues, leading them to most likely associate each other with "problems," "headaches," or "troubles").

2) Insensitivity to face needs (the subjects developed mutual dislike and loss of relational trust because of interactions that did not pay adequate attention to each others' face needs).

3) Inflexible conflict communication styles (driven by their individual face needs, one subject demonstrated increased dominance and intransigence in demands, exposing the other party to sensations of increasing worry and helplessness in trying to satisfy those demands. This led to mutual frustration and impatience, eroding the ability of both to handle conflict with each other).

Based on these findings, Chang (2011) makes four recommendations for intercultural communication:

1) Intercultural communicators should seek to recognize mutual face needs and engage in effective facework.

2) Intercultural communicators should seek to avoid interactions that are fueled by conflict, choosing instead to communicate with their counterparts under positive circumstances instead of merely when there is a problem.

3) Intercultural communicators should strive for interactional flexibility and vary their conflict communication styles to create a better fit with each relationship or situation, which entails a certain degree of cultural adaptation.

4) Intercultural communicators should be show adaptability toward their partners' systems of cultural meaning. Chang cites the work of Berry (1998) and Kim (1997, 2002) as evidence that, in the interest of productive interaction with members of the host culture, a person must be willing to look beyond their home cultural identity.

These concepts are vitally important to the purpose of the study at hand. While staff at Organization A's office in the United States issue directives in the mindset of their own home culture, these directives (which are generally conveyed via email) are received and interpreted by the communications coordinators in the setting of their own countries and cultures, and vice-versa. Therefore, a failure to anticipate and adapt the communication to the recipient's cultural framework and face needs can create and perpetuate misunderstandings that can effectively cripple and even destroy working relationships.

The methodology used in Chang's (2011) study (detailed analysis of written intercultural communication via email, based on existing research) appears sound. It is essentially the same methodology the author of this study will use to analyze the effects of culture on business communications at Organization A.

Murphy and Levy (2006) conducted a study on the effects of using the medium of electronic mail (email) on the degree of politeness used by communicators, with special regard for the effects of perceived impoliteness by the sender on the issue of face for the recipient. In particular, the study looked at how the writers incorporated politeness indicators in their emails. The research was carried out on a group of university academics in Australia and another in Korea. The primary focus was their email communications with colleagues overseas whom they had never personally met.

The methodology used for the study included gathering two sets of data. The first was a questionnaire administered to a random sample of 122 full-time faculty and staff at a university in Australia. Interviews and email text analysis were also used for data triangulation. The second was a smaller group of 16 Korean academics who had near-native proficiency in English and worked at seven universities in South Korea. Each of these respondents taught at least a portion of their courses in English and communicated internationally via email with English-speaking individuals. The Korean group's questionnaire was essentially identical to the one used for the Australians, although it was modified slightly for additional clarity. Both questionnaires posed the following questions:

1: In general, do you think you express politeness differently in your email communications with unknown receivers overseas compared to your email communications with people you know in Australia? (Korea)? Yes/No

If YES, how do you express politeness differently?

2: In your opinion, do you ever perceive a lack of politeness in the emails you receive from overseas? Yes/No

If YES, in what way?

3: In general, how do you show politeness in your overseas email communications?

Figure 2.2

Results of Survey in Politeness in Writing Emails
(Murphy & Levy, 2006)

Australia
• Politeness in email according to the Australian participants was incorporated in many elements of writing such as orthography, text structure, punctuation and clarity. • Formality, including formal greetings and closings, was an important way of showing politeness in overseas email communication; correct titles were important also. • Omission of certain written elements, for example, colloquialisms, jargon, and/or humor, could indicate politeness according to the participants.
Korea
• Formal language was an important politeness consideration, especially in terms of address at the beginning of an email. Conventional written protocol was often followed in Korean email texts. Some participants also said they saw a difference between levels of formality between Koreans writing to other Koreans and Koreans writing to non-Koreans. Correct titles were important also. • Face-saving language in email texts was

> considered important for politeness and the
> absence of it was seen as impolite.
>
> - Brief email texts were seen as impolite.
> - Indirect language for requests was considered polite. However, some participants said that they used direct language in email texts generally.
> - Modal verbs were preferred by some of the Korean participants to indicate politeness e.g., *would, could, and might*.
> - Interest by non-Koreans in the way things are done in Korea was also considered polite according to the participants.

The results of the study by Murphy and Levy (2006) seem to indicate that politeness is a very important consideration in intercultural email exchanges, so much so that a perceived lack of politeness can cause the recipient of the email to lose face (see Figure 1.2). Additionally, it demonstrates that individuals of differing cultural backgrounds expect different things from their email communication, and a failure to satisfy those expectations can negatively affect the communication process. This information is of great significance to the study at hand, because communication among members of Organization A's team of field correspondents is more often than not carried out between or among individuals of different nationalities and cultures.

Conclusion

The literature reviewed presents a broad consensus in support of the idea that culture greatly influences the effectiveness of communication. Culture is defined as the sum of a people's learned behavior patterns, attitudes, and material things (Hall, 1959, 1973). It is also described as a series of situational models for behavior and thought (Hall, 1976, 1981); the way in which a group of people solves problems and reconciles dilemmas (Trompenaars & Hampden-Turner, 1998; Schein, 1985); and the collective programming of the mind which distinguishes one group or category of people from another (McFarlin & Sweeney, 2006; Hofstede, 1993). Culture is critical to effective communication, especially as relates to non-verbal behavior (Shi & Fan, 2010).

Jameson (2007) suggests that a critical factor in intercultural communications is to be aware of one's true level of (or lack of) knowledge about others, and to adjust the schemata each communicator has of other cultures as communication occurs. She also warns against confusing culture with nationality. Holliday (2010) performed research that challenges the notion of variability in communication due to cultural factors, but his sample was so small and his methodology so questionable that his findings carry little credibility.

Bennett (1998) contends that understanding, appreciating and respecting the idea of difference is critical to intercultural communication, while Nordby (2008) holds out little hope for the success of intercultural communication in instances where the communicators fail to distinguish between culturally-shaped values and beliefs or thoughts.

Research by Campbell (2008) found that intercultural communication via electronic means such as electronic mail (email) is even more challenging than other forms of intercultural communication, because the absence of non-verbal aspects of communication diminishes the accuracy of message interpretation when compared to a face-to-face setting. Participants in her study also found that being physically separated from their partners in the study meant they could not prompt each other to answer questions.

Cultural concepts are by definition generalizations, and it is impossible to discuss cultures without generalizing; however, not every individual within a culture will conform exactly to the cultural generalization. This does not mean that the generalizations are incorrect; it simply means that a given trait seems to predominate within a specified culture (Storti, 1994).

Major cultural concepts include individualism/collectivism, context, face, uncertainty avoidance, masculinity/femininity, harmony, concepts of time and power distance (Hall (1976, 1981); Hall (1983); Trompenaars & Hampden-Turner (1998); Hofstede, 2009; Samovar, Porter & McDaniel (2009). All of these are important to intercultural communication.

Gudykunst (1997) concludes that, while certain aspects of cultural variability are stronger in different cultures, it is impossible to fully understand variations and similarities in communications among cultures using a single cultural variability aspect; rather, this requires different combinations of variability aspects. These aspects include individualism-collectivism, uncertainty avoidance, power distance and masculinity-femininity. Context is another cultural aspect; Martin, Hammer & Bradford (1994) found that contextual dimensions may influence different cultural groups' judgments differently for some behaviors; in other words, behavioral expectations may differ depending on whether one is operating within or outside of one's own cultural group. Meanwhile, Olk (2009) explored the challenges posed to oral and written communication by cultural variability. He found that a lack of understanding of cultural references can greatly impact the degree of comprehension on the part of the recipient. Seo,

Miller, Schmidt and Sowa (2008) observed that a culture's collectivist or individualist tendency has a significant bearing on how issues of conflict are addressed, especially when it comes to the ability or willingness to say "no."

Chang's (2011) work reveals that face is an important consideration in intercultural communication via email. He observes that face-based goal issues, if not properly managed, can lead to unresolved conflicts. Meanwhile, Murphy and Levy (2006) found that the issue of politeness is so important to intercultural email communications that a perceived lack of politeness can cause the recipient of the email to lose face. They also discovered that people from different cultures expect different things from their email communication, and a failure to satisfy those expectations can negatively affect the communication process.

Overall, the methodologies used in the studies reviewed seem to be sound and to utilize accepted statistical procedures. However, a methodological weakness common to many of the studies lies in their small sample sizes. Clearly, it would be impossible to survey the entire population of intercultural business communicators, but the fact that the population is so disconnected and dispersed means most research will be limited to small samples. But despite the lack of statistical significance of the individual studies, taken as a whole they provide a good sense of the fact that culture is a distinct factor to be reckoned with when people of different cultures communicate.

Chapter 3: Assumptions and Methodology

Based on the abundance of existing research on the subject of the effects of culture on communication as a whole, it seems natural to assume that the participants in this study should reflect the characteristics of the larger population. The work of Hall (1959, 1973, 1976, 1981, 1983; Hall & Hall, 1990), Hofstede (1980, 2009), and others establishes with considerable authority that national culture does indeed affect interpersonal communications to a marked degree. In fact, Hofstede (2009) gives the United States an individualism (IDV) score of 91%; Trompenaars & Hampden-Turner (1998, p. 52) give the U.S. a somewhat lower yet still strong individualism score of 69%. While IDV scores are not available for all of the countries where Organization A has field agencies, a mean IDV score taken from the countries for which a rating does exist comes in at 30%. This is based on 21% for all of Latin America (scores are not available for many of the individual countries in question), 32% for the Philippines, 40% for India, and 27% for Zambia (Hofstede, 2009). Because a composite mean is being used for non-U.S. countries, this study will use as its measurement of IDV for the United States the mean of the U.S. IDV scores from Hofstede (2009) and Trompenaars & Hampden-Turner (1998, p. 52), which is 80%.

Hypotheses

Qualitative: The investigator will identify by observation, interview, and through the gathering of exploratory information the components of a cross-cultural communications network as well as an instrument and methodology for paradigmatic research.

Quantitative:

- Null hypothesis (H_0): IDV scores for respondents will show no variability based on national culture between Group A and Group B greater than would be expected by chance.
- Alternative hypothesis (H_1): IDV scores for respondents will vary significantly between Group A and Group B, indicating that the role of culture in interpersonal business communication is indeed significant.

Given the small sample sizes and exploratory nature of the survey instrument used in this study, the results of this study may be suggestive at best. It is hoped they will provide insight into specific communication problems and opportunities that may exist within Organization A, and to which cultural principles established through the body of existing research may be applied in an effort to discover practical solutions.

Methodology

The methodology selected for the research was a purposive qualitative study containing a prototype quantitative design. Purposive sampling was chosen because the intent was to measure cultural dimensions within the context of specific groups instead of the general population; therefore, random sampling would have been inappropriate. The research performed in this study is intended to give a better idea of the cultural views of the specific respondents to the study. This would be done in hopes of crafting an internal communication strategy customized to the specific needs of Organization A.

Research Instruments

The study was conducted in three phases, with the first research instrument consisting of an eight-question survey (see Appendix A), which was slightly modified for Groups C and D as mentioned below (see Appendix B). This survey was used for phases 1 and 2.

- Phase 1 consisted of having two groups (hereafter referred to as Group A and Group B) within Organization A complete and return the survey via email. Group A was comprised of members of the Creative Services department at Organization A's home office in the United States. Group B consisted of communications coordinators at Organization A's field agencies around the world. Nations represented in the makeup of Group B included Chile, Colombia, the Dominican Republic, Ecuador, Guatemala, Honduras, India, the Philippines and Zambia. A total of 6 respondents participated in Group A, while Group B included 13 respondents.

- Phase 2 consisted of polling two outside groups that were completely devoid of connection to groups A and B, but shared similar characteristics: for example, all worked in the not-for-profit sector. These were labeled Group C and Group D. Group C consisted of 11 evangelical ministers located across the United States. Group D was made up of 36 evangelical ministers in Peru. While most members of Group C were not affiliated with any particular denomination but shared virtually identical beliefs and religious values, all 36 respondents in Peru were members of a religious organization known as *Iglesia Cristiana Apostólica Pentecostal* (Christian Apostolic Pentecostal Church). This religious organization embraced essentially identical values and beliefs to those shared by Group C in the United States. Groups C and D were administered the same survey as Groups A and B; only minor alterations were made to job titles and tasks referenced within the survey, for the purpose of relevance to their working environments. Surveys were collected from Group C via email, while surveys were administered to Group D in a live meeting.

- Phase 3 was only administered to groups A and B. This phase consisted of having respondents write an email assigning a particular task to the communications coordinators of Organization A. For this assignment, each respondent played the role of Organization A's Field Content Manager, who is the author of this study. The purpose of the exercise was to observe differences in the structure and content of the emails that would indicate significant correlations or culture-based differences in communication style between the groups.

Survey Instrument – Phases 1 and 2

The survey instrument used in phases 1 and 2 consisted of eight simulated scenarios in which the communications coordinator receives a message from the Field Content Manager at Organization A's home office (or, in the case of Phase 2, job titles and terminology are altered only enough to create a scenario that is relevant to the two groups of ministers). Two possible responses were provided for each simulation, and the respondent was asked to select the response that most closely reflected his or her probable reaction to the message.

- Scenario 1 (Q1)

  "We are concerned because lately we have noticed a marked increase in the number of story ideas and follow-ups that are being submitted late. Please remember that it is critical that you submit your material on time. Late submissions cannot be tolerated." The respondent is one of the communications coordinators who have been submitting work late.

  o Response A

    "I need to work on getting my assignments in on time. If I don't, I may be reprimanded."

  o Response B

    "It seems a lot of us are having the same problem. My fellow communications coordinators and I should talk about the problem and see what we can do to fix it."

Rationale

Q1 was intended to determine whether the respondent thought independently or consultatively. Response A would indicate an inclination toward independent action, which speaks of individualism; Response B, on the other hand, shows a tendency toward consultative problem solving, which can indicate communitarianism (Trompenaars & Hampden-Turner, 1998, p. 62). Thus a response of "A" would be counted as an individualistic response, and "B" would be considered communitarian.

- Scenario 2 (Q2)

  "We are concerned because lately we have noticed a marked increase in the number of story ideas and follow-ups that are being submitted late. Please remember that it is critical that you submit your material on time. Late submissions cannot be tolerated." The respondent is not a communications coordinator who has been submitting work late.

  o Response A

    You email back immediately to remind the content manager that you are usually, if not always, punctual with your assignments.

- o Response B

  You say nothing, because you realize that although you are punctual, others on the team may not always be; therefore, it seems reasonable that the entire team should be admonished.

  Rationale

  Q2 measures whether the respondent feels more responsibility as an individual or as a member of a group. Response A reveals individualistic tendencies, or the belief that the individual committing the failure is responsible, while response B indicates the more communitarian view that, because the individual works in a team, the responsibility should be carried by the group (Trompenaars & Hampden-Turner, 1998, p. 56).

- Scenario 3 (Q3)

  "Yesterday was the deadline for XYZ project. Thanks to all of you who submitted your assignments. So far, we have only received submissions from the following agencies: ABC, DEF and GHI." The respondent is the communications coordinator from agency ABC.

  - o Response A

    "It makes me feel good that my hard work on this assignment is recognized.

I'm glad the email mentions that I have already submitted; I would hate for anyone to think I was late."

o Response B
"Wow...I wish the email hadn't mentioned me specifically. The other communications coordinators who are late must feel terrible."

Rationale

Q3 is designed to measure the respondent's perspective on recognition. McFarlin & Sweeney (2006, p. 357) observe that in individualistic cultures, individual performance is important and should be rewarded on the basis of deservingness, while in more collectivist cultures rewards are "more likely to be distributed equally, regardless of performance, to preserve group harmony and cohesiveness." As a matter of personal experience, the author of this study found a subordinate from a highly collectivist culture to be reluctant to accept a significant promotion out of concern for the feelings of the other group members who were not being promoted. Therefore, a more individualistic respondent could be expected to choose Response A, while a collectivist might favor Response B.

- Scenario 4 (Q4)

  "Yesterday was the deadline for XYZ project. Thanks to all of you who submitted your assignments. So far, we have only received submissions from the following agencies: ABC, DEF and GHI." The respondent is the communications coordinator for an agency that has not yet submitted.

  o Response A

    "I feel humiliated. This email has embarrassed me in front of all my colleagues."

  o Response B

    "It's only fair that those who met the deadline be named. After all, they worked hard to get their work in on time, so it would not be fair for them to be reprimanded along with everyone else."

Rationale

Q4 seeks to learn the respondent's orientation to face. "Face" refers to the culturally variable need for self-respect, pride and dignity (McFarlin & Sweeney, 2006, p. 173). In cultures where face is a significant concern, there are two aspects of loss of face that people seek to avoid: losing face oneself, and causing others to lose face (McFarlin & Sweeney, 2006, p. 174). The premise on which this scenario advances is that a respondent from a collectivist, face-sensitive culture would be more likely to choose Response A, while an individualist could be expected to favor Response B. Given that in each of the previous three questions the individualistic response was listed first, the order of responses was reversed in this scenario to attempt to mitigate any halo effect.

- Scenario 5 (Q5)

  "Yesterday was the deadline for XYZ project. Thanks to all of you who submitted your assignments. So far, we have only received submissions from the following agencies: ABC, DEF and GHI." The respondent is the communications coordinator from agency ABC.

  o Response A

    "I'm glad they mentioned that I turned my work in on time. I feel sorry for the other communications coordinators, but it's important for my boss to know I'm doing my job."

  o Response B

    "Wow...I wish the email hadn't mentioned me specifically. I hope this doesn't cause the other communications coordinators to feel badly toward me."

Rationale

Q5 is designed to assess a combination of the respondent's attitude toward face and his or her sense of responsibility to the group. Response A explores the respondent's need to reassure the supervisor of the acceptability of his or her individual performance, while in Response B is concerned with the loss of face the respondent's colleagues might experience as a consequence. An individualistic respondent might be expected to select Response A, while a collectivist, face-oriented respondent with a strong sense of responsibility to the group should gravitate toward Response B.

- Scenario 6 (Q6)

  "Yesterday was the deadline for XYZ project. Thanks to all of you who submitted your assignments. So far, we have only received submissions from the following agencies: ABC, DEF and GHI." The respondent is the communications coordinator for an agency that has not yet submitted.

  o Response A

    "I'm really not concerned about my boss seeing that I haven't submitted this project yet. If he/she asks me about it,

I'll explain how busy I've been with other critical projects, and he/she will understand."

- o Response B
  "I wish the email would have been more general, and I wish our bosses hadn't been copied. I'm afraid this will hurt my agency director's confidence in me, even though I have been buried in critical projects."

Rationale

Q6 deals specifically with the issue of preserving or losing face before one's supervisor. In less face-oriented cultures, which tend to be individualistic, one could expect the respondent to be less concerned with losing face if legitimate issues underlay his or her lateness in submitting the required materials; the respondent would simply explain to the supervisor the extenuating circumstances, and there would be no negative reflection on his or her personal image. However, in a face-oriented culture, for one's boss to be made aware of an apparent failure or shortcoming could be devastating, as illustrated by Ho, Fu & Ng (2004). For Q6, an individualist could be expected to select Response A, and a collectivist might favor Response B.

- Scenario 7 (Q7)

  "This is just a reminder that the deadline for project XYZ is approaching. Please be certain that all materials for the project are submitted on or before the due date."

  o Response A

    "Deadlines are important, but many other factors come into play in carrying out a project. I will turn in the project as close to the deadline as possible, but it's only reasonable to understand that circumstances in the field may cause it to be a day or two late."

  o Response B

    "This project must be turned in exactly by the due date. Being on time is so important that I will work extra hours in the evenings and on weekends if necessary to meet the deadline."

  Rationale

  Q7 aims to probe whether the respondent regards time in a monochronic or polychronic fashion. Trompenaars & Hampden-Turner (1998, p. 128) refer to these same concepts as *sequential* and *synchronic* time, pointing out that sequential or monochronic individuals operate under tight schedules and view a lack of punctuality as rude. Synchronic or polychronic people, on the other hand, are less insistent on punctuality – not because the passage of time is unimportant, but because other cultural values vie with punctuality. They further observe that it is not that people in synchronic or polychronic cultures are unable to meet deadlines; rather, they prefer to follow the subjective time of the relationship over the objective time of the clock, because they are more people-oriented than task-oriented (Trompenaars & Hampden-Turner, 1998, p. 141). Based on this, people from monochronic or sequential cultures could be expected to select Response B, while those from more polychronic or synchronous cultures should prefer Response A. Note that once again the individualist and collectivist answers were transposed to reduce the likelihood of a halo effect.

- Scenario 8 (Q8)
  "Project XYZ is extremely critical and takes top priority over any other projects you are working on. If you have other projects that are in conflict with this project, please let me know and I will be happy to contact your agency director to help reprioritize your assignments."

o <u>Response A</u>

"It would be very helpful for the content manager to contact my agency director to explain why this project is more important than anything else I am working on."

o <u>Response B</u>

"I would prefer to reprioritize my assignments myself, even if it means working overtime to complete all my projects. When I receive special intervention from the home office, it makes my coworkers at the agency feel resentful toward me."

<u>Rationale</u>

Q8 addresses two culturally important concepts: time management practices and ingroup bias. While in monochronic cultures it is common for supervisors to become involved with scheduling subordinates' work at a task level, in polychronic cultures "for an employer to schedule a subordinate's work for him would be considered a tyrannical violation of his individuality – an invasion of the self" (Hall, 1983, p. 50). And the author's personal experience supports the idea that in collectivist cultures that favor the ingroup, members of the ingroup may experience feelings of resentment toward outside interference, especially if this interference seems to favor one member of the ingroup over the others. Therefore, respondents from individualistic cultures could be expected to choose Response A, and those from collectivist cultures should logically prefer Response B.

While some inferential statistics would be used simply to test for any basic correlations among variables, the design of phases 1 and 2 of the study was primarily qualitative, utilizing purposive rather than random samples. Descriptive statistics would be generated to compare responses among groups, rather than engage in the more advanced inferential analysis that would be required were this study seminal in nature.

Email Assignment – Phase 3

The third phase of the study involved only groups A and B, asking each respondent to craft an email assigning a task to the communications coordinators. This email assignment was based on real-life task assignments sent regularly to the communications coordinators by the Content Manager at the home office. All participants in groups A and B received the following instructions:

Imagine you are the content manager at Organization A. You are writing an email to all communications coordinators to give them an assignment with the following characteristics:

- *The assignment name is Project XYZ.*
- *The due date for the project is August 31, 2011.*
- *The assignment is for XYZ magazine; therefore, the due date is __extremely critical and inflexible__.*
- *All photos must be of the highest quality. Any photos not meeting minimum quality standards will be rejected. Because of the critical nature of this project, a failure to deliver quality photos by the due date could carry serious implications for the communications coordinator, up to and including termination.*
- *Communication with the project owner (in this case, the content manager) is absolutely essential so he can be aware of any conditions or situations that might threaten to make the project late.*
- *The communications coordinators must submit their assignments to the proper category in the CSS [Content*

Submission System] and must notify the project owner when the assignment has been submitted.

Please write a brief, concise email that assigns the above project to all communications coordinators (CCs) in a way that communicates the urgency of meeting the quality standards and the deadline, but at the same time respects the professional dignity of the CCs. Your email should point out all of the above-mentioned project characteristics in a way that is frank but not offensive.

The design of the email project was purely qualitative. The emails would be manually analyzed to identify three specific trends: 1) a preponderance of usage of "I" versus "we" to identify whether the authors tended toward individualism or communitarianism in their writing style; 2) whether the respondent dealt directly or indirectly with having to threaten discipline (a conflict-avoidant style would be characteristic of a collectivist, high-context culture (McFarlin & Sweeney, 2006, p. 219)); and 3) whether the respondent was more task-oriented or people-oriented (individualists tend to be more task-oriented (Trompenaars & Hampden-Turner, 1998, pp. 126-128)). Differences in the average scores of each of these categories would be analyzed for statistical significance using the Fisher Exact Test, and descriptive statistics would be generated from the findings. From there, using the known nuances associated with these two cultural aspects and given the quality of existing research by the likes of Hall, Hofstede, Gudykunst, Trompenaars, etc., the existing literature would be used to create intraorganizational communication guidelines for Organization A.

Limitations

There are a number of limitations that could affect the validity of the participants' responses.

- With the exception of the respondents of Group C, all participants were drawn from within specific organizations.
- Both of these organizations have had multicultural and multinational influences for many years.
- Because of their prolonged exposure to different cultures, participants may have already experienced some level of adaptation to other cultures; therefore, their responses might not be reflective of the degrees of cultural difference that might be in evidence were the study to have been conducted on a truly random sample that lacked the organizational background of the current respondents.

- The respondents from groups C and D are strongly influenced by common religious beliefs. Trompenaars & Hampden-Turner (1998, p. 56) establish that it is necessary to identify the community a given culture agrees with, as any number of communities or groups may wield a stronger influence than others. In the case of groups C and D, it is quite possible that the effects of their shared religious values and beliefs would override the influence of their respective national cultures.

Chapter 4: Results and Discussion

Due to the relatively small sample sizes, the Fisher Exact Test was used to determine statistical significance of the differences in responses generated by the survey instrument used in phases 1 and 2. The mean of the responses was also calculated for each group.

Phase 1

The Fisher Exact Test revealed few statistically significant differences among the responses from the groups. Group A, the team at the home office of Organization A in the United States, was tested against Group B (the communications coordinators in Asia, Africa and Latin America). See Table 4.1 for the statistical analysis of the results, in which no differences were statistically significant. For average individualism (IND) scores, see Figure 4.1.

Table 4.1

Average Individualism (IND) Scores and Fisher Exact Test P Values for Group A versus Group B

Item	Avg. IND Score for Both	Avg. IND Score for Group	Avg. IND Score for Group	Two-Tailed P Value

	Groups	A	B	
Q1 -	Independent versus consultative style	43.59	33.33	53.85	0.6285
Q2 -	Individual versus group responsibility	16.03	16.67	15.38	1.0000
Q3 -	Orientation toward individual recognition	88.46	100.00	76.92	0.5170
Q4 -	Orientation to face	80.77	100.00	61.54	0.1280
Q5 -	Attitude toward face and responsibility to group	76.28	83.33	69.23	1.0000
Q6 -	Face before supervisor	43.59	33.33	53.85	0.6285
Q7 -	Time (monochronism versus polychronism)	80.13	83.33	76.92	1.0000
Q8 -	Time management and ingroup bias	68.59	83.33	53.85	0.3331

Note: Avg. IND Score for Both Groups = mean of all IND scores for Group A and Group B, expressed as a percentage of total responses; Avg. IND Score for Group A = mean of all IND scores

115

for Group A; Avg. IND Score for Group B = mean of all IND scores for Group B; Two-Tailed P Value derived using Fisher Exact Test ("Analyze a 2x2," 2005) to compensate for small sample sizes. Confidence level for Fisher Exact Test is 95%. * = statistically significant.

Figure 4.1

Average IND Scores for Groups A and B

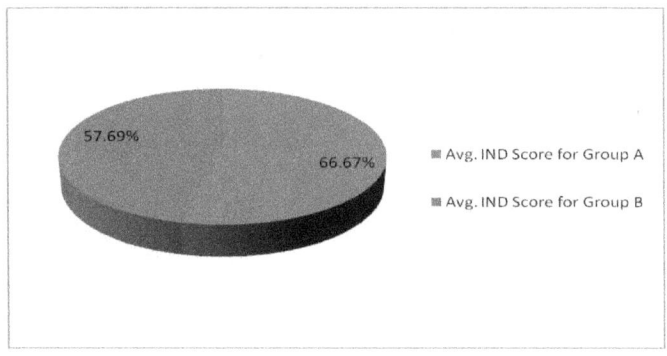

Phase 2

The results for Phase 2 were similar to those of Phase 1 (see Table 4.2). The differences in responses between groups C and D (the ministers from the United States and Peru) also failed to show statistical significance, with the exception of Q5.

Table 4.2

Average Individualism (IND) Scores and Fisher Exact Test P Values for Group C vs. Group D

Item	Avg. IND Score for	Avg. IND	Avg. IND	Two-Tailed

		Both Groups	Score for Group C	Score for Group D	P Value
Q1 -	Independent versus consultative style	64.15	72.73	55.56	0.4850
Q2 -	Individual versus group responsibility	31.31	18.18	44.44	0.1644
Q3 -	Orientation toward individual recognition	36.24	36.36	36.11	1.0000
Q4 -	Orientation to face	43.18	36.36	50.00	0.4908
Q5 -	Attitude toward face and responsibility to group	38.26	18.18	58.33	0.0351*
Q6 -	Face before supervisor	37.63	36.36	38.89	1.0000
Q7 -	Time (monochronism versus polychronism)	67.56	54.55	80.56	0.1176
Q8 -	Time management and ingroup bias	60.61	54.55	66.67	0.4766

Note: Avg. IND Score for Both Groups = mean of all IND scores for Group C and Group D, expressed as a percentage of total responses; Avg. IND Score for Group C = mean of all IND scores for Group C; Avg. IND Score for Group D = mean of all IND scores for Group D; Two-Tailed P Value derived using Fisher Exact Test ("Analyze a 2x2," 2005) to compensate for small sample sizes. Confidence level for Fisher Exact Test is 95%. * = statistically significant.

Figure 4.2

Average IND Scores for Groups C and D

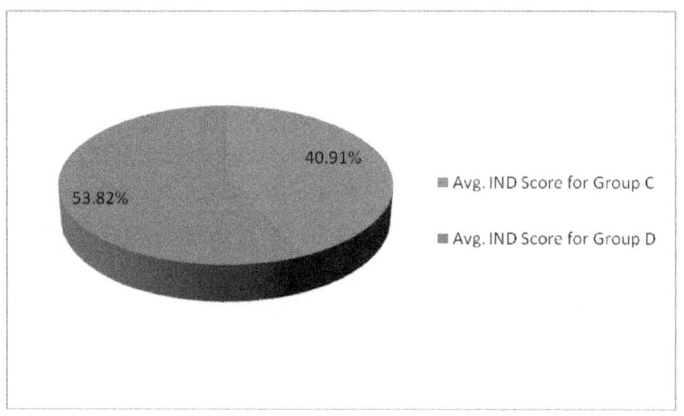

The results of the surveys of Groups A, B, C and D failed to produce results capable of rejecting the null hypothesis. However, the instrument used was exploratory, technically deficient and lacking in documented reliability and validity. A comparison of its results to established data from respected studies such as the one conducted by Trompenaars & Hampden-Turner (1998) casts serious doubt upon its reliability, as the survey instrument in question failed to consistently identify predicted differences that could reasonably be expected to be present. Based on the author's personal experience, qualitative observations and the dramatically different results obtained in Phase 3, it seems likely an instrument could be developed with better technical characteristics, measured reliability and, at a minimum, construct validity. It is the author's belief that such an instrument would have a strong likelihood of testing and successfully supporting the alternative hypothesis once design flaws were eliminated.

Phase 3

This phase consisted of asking the respondents from Group A and Group B to write an email assuming the role of the content manager and assigning a task to the communications coordinators. The task would contain very specific instructions and would ask the writer to specify that a failure to meet established deadlines and quality levels would result in severe disciplinary action, up to and including termination of employment. These characteristics would be used to determine the respondent's level of individualism.

The first comparison was made between Group A and Group B as a whole. The results were strongly statistically significant (see Table 4.3 and figures 4.3, 4.4 and 4.5).

Table 4.3

Average Individualism, Confrontation-Avoidance and Task-Orientation Scores and Fisher Exact Test P Values for Group A vs. Group B

	Item	Average Score for Group A	Average Score for Group B	Two-Tailed P Value
Q1 -	Individualism versus collectivism	66.67	47.14	0.0065**
Q2 -	Direct approach to confrontation versus indirect approach	83.33	33.33	0.0002***
Q3 -	Task-orientation vs. people-orientation	100.00	33.33	0.0001***

Note: Avg. IND Avg. IND Score for Group A = mean of all IND scores for Group A; Avg. IND Score for Group B = mean of all IND scores for Group B; Two-Tailed P Value derived using Fisher Exact Test ("Analyze a 2x2," 2005) to compensate for small sample sizes. Confidence level for Fisher Exact Test is 95%. * = statistically significant; ** = very statistically significant; *** = extremely statistically significant.

Figure 4.3

Individualism scores for Group A vs. Group B in Phase 3

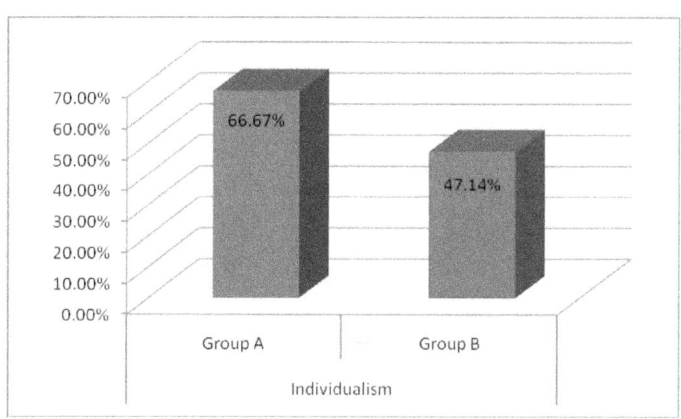

Figure 4.4

Scores for directly and indirectly addressing
confrontation for Group A vs. Group B in Phase 3

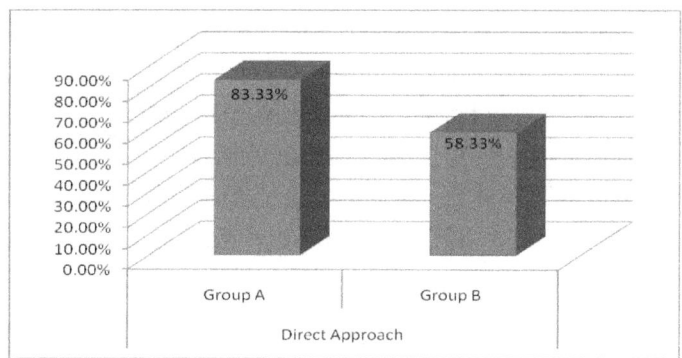

Figure 4.5

Scores for task orientation and people orientation for
Group A vs. Group B in Phase 3

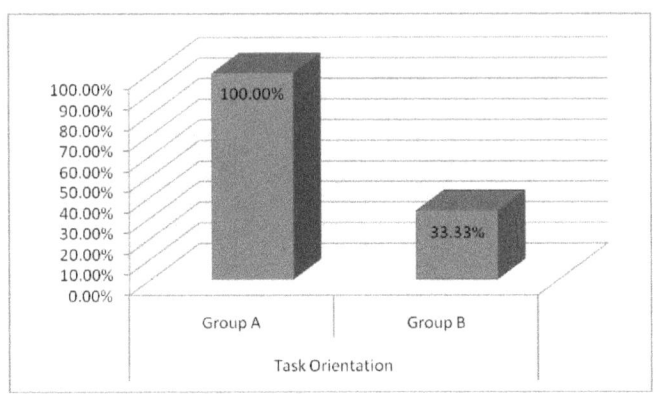

The statistical significance of the differences
between Group A and Group B appears to be virtually
unassailable. However, the author wished to further
analyze the responses to determine if any marked
differences exist among the various geographical
regions making up Group B. Therefore, the same tests
that were run between Group A and Group B were
conducted testing Group A against the respondents
from Asia, which include three from the Philippines
and one from India. The results (see Table 4.4 and
figures 4.6, 4.7 and 4.8) were surprising in that the
respondents from Asia scored significantly higher in
individualism than their counterparts in the United
States in two of three areas covered by the analysis.
The author suspects that this may stem in part from the

fact that both the Philippines and India use English on a widespread basis, and both nations have been heavily exposed to Western culture.

Table 4.4

Average Individualism, Confrontation-Avoidance and Task-Orientation Scores and Fisher Exact Test P Values for Group A vs. Asia

Item	Average Score for Group A	Average Score for Asia	Two-Tailed P Value
Q1 - Individualism versus collectivism	66.67	75.00	0.2753
Q2 - Direct approach to confrontation versus indirect approach	83.33	100.00	0.0001***
Q3 - Task-orientation vs. people-orientation	100.00	100.00	1.0000

Note: Avg. IND Avg. IND Score for Group A = mean of all IND scores for Group A; Avg. IND Score for Group B = mean of all IND scores for Group B; Two-Tailed P Value derived using Fisher Exact Test ("Analyze a 2x2," 2005) to compensate for small sample sizes. Confidence level for Fisher Exact Test is 95%. * = statistically significant; ** = very statistically significant; *** = extremely statistically significant.

Figure 4.6

Individualism scores for Group A vs. Asia in Phase 3

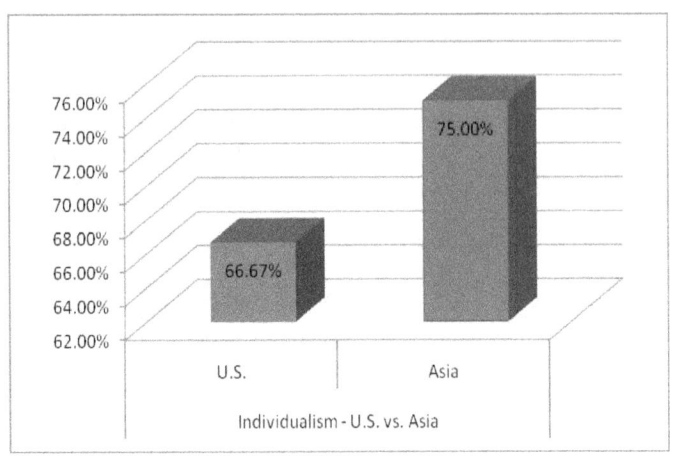

Figure 4.7

Scores for directly and indirectly addressing
confrontation for Group A vs. Asia in Phase 3

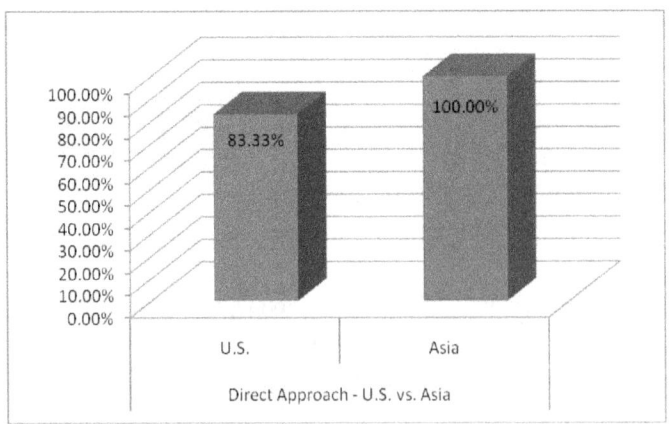

Figure 4.8

Scores for task orientation and people orientation for Group A vs. Asia in Phase 3

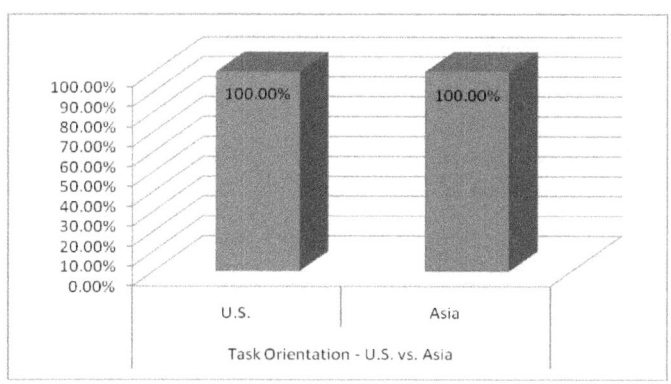

Instead, the results for Group A were compared to the responses from Latin America (see Table 4.5 and Figures 4.9, 4.10 and 4.11). Markedly significant differences were found.

Table 4.5

Average Individualism, Confrontation-Avoidance and Task-Orientation Scores and Fisher Exact Test P Values for Group A vs. Latin America

Item	Average Score for Group A	Average Score for Latin America	Two-Tailed P Value

Q1 -	Individualism versus collectivism	66.67	34.88	0.0001***
Q2 -	Direct approach to confrontation versus indirect approach	83.33	28.57	0.0001***
Q3 -	Task-orientation vs. people-orientation	100.00	0.00	0.0001***

Note: Avg. IND Avg. IND Score for Group A = mean of all IND scores for Group A; Avg. IND Score for Group B = mean of all IND scores for Group B; Two-Tailed P Value derived using Fisher Exact Test ("Analyze a 2x2," 2005) to compensate for small sample sizes. Confidence level for Fisher Exact Test is 95%. * = statistically significant; ** = very statistically significant; *** = extremely statistically significant.

Figure 4.9

Individualism scores for Group A vs. Latin America in Phase 3

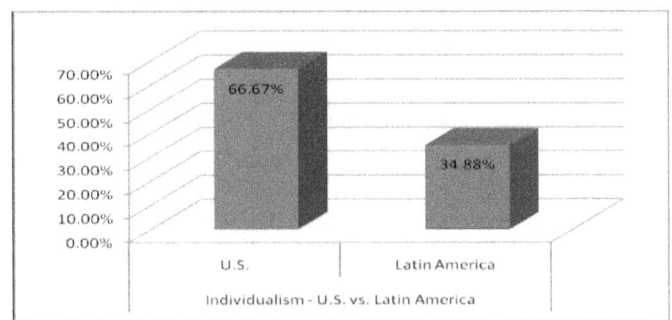

Figure 4.10

Scores for directly and indirectly addressing
confrontation for Group A vs. Latin America in Phase 3

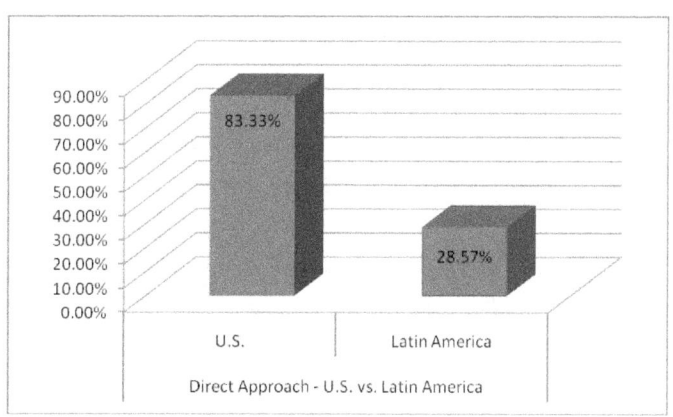

Figure 4.11

Scores for task orientation and people orientation for
Group A vs. Latin America in Phase 3

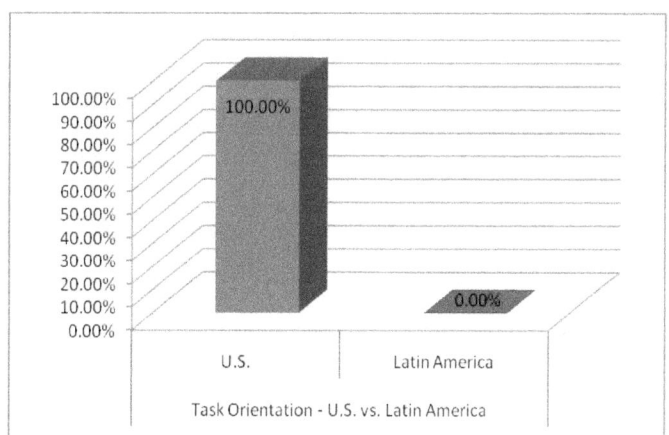

No testing was performed in isolation on the data from Africa, as there was only one respondent from the region, which rendered it impossible to obtain a mean score for comparison. Instead, the response from Africa was factored into the overarching comparison between Group A and Group B.

Summary

The overall IDV scores for Phase 3 were calculated by obtaining the mean of the Individualism, Conflict Avoidance and Task/People Orientation scores for Groups A and B. The overall IDV scores for these were, respectively, 83.33% and 37.93% (Figure 4.12). A Fisher Exact Test analysis revealed that neither of these constituted a statistically significant difference from the baseline score of 80% IDV for Group A and 30% IDV for Group B that was calculated from the research of Hall (1959, 1973, 1976, 1981, 1983; Hall & Hall, 1990), Hofstede (1980, 2009) and Trompenaars & Hampden-Turner (1998).

Figure 4.12

Overall IDV scores for Group A and Group B in Phase 3

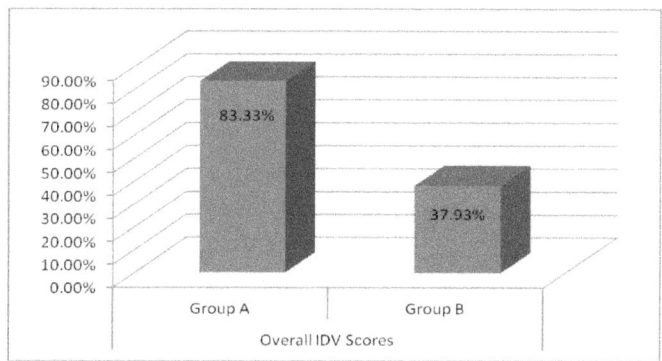

In summary, the research project yielded the following results:

- The results of the survey questionnaire used in phases 1 and 2 are deemed unreliable due to possible design flaws in the survey instrument; as a result, they were not taken into consideration

- Phase 3, the email writing exercise, produced results that the author considers to be reliable for the following reasons:
  - The situation was much less theoretical than that posed by the survey instrument, because participants were involved in crafting an email of a type regularly used in their daily work
  - Because the email writing assignment was free-form, less opportunity existed

for the participants to attempt to guess what responses were desired from them

- o The results were quite consistent with the established individualism scores derived from the work of respected researchers such as Hall (1959, 1973, 1976, 1981, 1983; Hall & Hall, 1990), Hofstede (1980, 2009) and Trompenaars & Hampden-Turner (1998).
- o Group A tested strongly individualistic and Group B scored strongly collectivist, although the Asia subgroup of Group B was even more strongly individualistic than Group A.

- Therefore, based on the results of Phase 3, the null hypothesis was rejected and the alternative hypothesis was accepted.

Chapter 5: Conclusions and Recommendations

The research in this study was conducted primarily to confirm that culturally-based differences existed between the communication styles of Group A and Group B, both internal to Organization A, and to verify that the two groups scored reasonably close to the national averages for their respective countries on the cultural tests for individualism conducted by Hall (1959, 1973, 1976, 1981, 1983; Hall & Hall, 1990), Hofstede (1980, 2009) and Trompenaars & Hampden-Turner (1998). Once it was determined that a particular group was primarily either individualistic or collectivist, the known cultural associations of these groups (high/low context, monochronicity/polychronicity, uncertainty avoidance, etc.) would be used to create a handbook for intercultural communication within the organization.

Conclusions

The scores of Group A and Group B would not be determined using existing instruments; rather, the instruments would be developed specifically for this study. Accordingly, the two primary instruments were created: an 8-question survey for phases 1 and 2 of the project, and an email-writing assignment for Phase 3. Following analysis of the data, recommendations would be made to improve communication among team members from different cultures. To supplement the information gleaned from the survey responses of groups A and B, a virtually identical survey was administered to Group C (a group of ministers in the United States) and Group D (a group of ministers in Peru).

The data gathered through the survey proved to be unreliable, failing to produce statistically significant differences and casting doubt on the reliability of the survey instrument. Therefore, the results for phases 1 and 2 were not taken into consideration in the final analysis of this project. However, the email-writing assignment, Phase 3, provided much more meaningful data with highly statistically significant differences between Group A and Group B.

The initial comparisons pitted Group A (Organization A's U.S.-based team) against Group B, comprised of communications coordinators from 10 countries outside the U.S.: Chile, Colombia, Ecuador, Dominican Republic, Guatemala, Honduras, India, Mexico, the Philippines and Zambia. The differences between the two groups were marked; Group A had more occurrences of the word "I" (indicating individualism), while Group B used "we" more frequently, giving Group A an individualism score of 66.67%, while Group B's was 47.14%. This created a strongly statistically significant two-tailed P value of 0.0065. Group A scored 83.33% on directly approaching the unpleasant subject of potential dismissal of an employee, while Group B scored only 58.33%. In some cases, respondents in Group B completely avoided addressing the negative consequence, preferring positive reinforcement of the importance of the project. Finally, 100% of respondents from Group A focused entirely on the task being assigned in the email, with little or no expression of warmth or recognition of the reader's humanity, while 66.67% of respondents from Group B took the time to compliment the reader and provide a strongly emotional rationale for the human impact of the task. All of these factors are typical of the expected cultural predispositions based on existing research; culturally, Group A was expected to be task-oriented, while Group B would likely be people-oriented.

This raised a question in the researcher's mind as to whether significant cultural subgroups existed within Group B because of its broad national composition. A comparison between the United States and Asia revealed the surprising fact that the Asian communications coordinators seemed to use a communication style that was even more individualistic than their American colleagues. The Asians scored 75% on individualism, as opposed to

66.67% for the Americans. The Asians also took a more direct approach to confrontation, scoring 100% versus 83.33% for the Americans. The two groups tied at 100% task orientation. Given the fact that established research classifies most of Asia as collectivist and high-context, the high individualism score for the Asian communications coordinators seems to offer an interesting avenue for future research. Two possible explanations are that 1) all Asian communications coordinators share a common language (English) with the home office in the United States, making it more likely that their communication style would eventually be influenced by their colleagues in America; and 2) India has a long history of British colonialism and the Philippines were closely allied with the United States for many years, which again raises the probability that their cultures and communication styles have been more heavily influenced by Western culture than those of other Asian nations.

Organization A only has one communications coordinator in Africa, so it was impossible to do a meaningful comparison between scores for the United States and for Africa. In Latin America, however, the contrast in communication styles was striking. Latin American CCs were heavily collectivist, with a score of 65.12% to just 33.33% collectivist for the team in the United States. They also proved to be heavily conflict-avoidant, scoring only 28.57% on a direct approach to confrontation versus 83.33% for Americans. The difference in orientation was just as marked; while Americans were 100% task-oriented, Latin Americans were 100% people-oriented.

Recommendations

The presence of such striking dissimilarities in communication styles within the global communications team implies significant challenges for Organization A. Given that the bulk of the organization's work (not just that of its Creative Services department) is conducted in the international arena, the ability to communicate clearly and effectively across cultural boundaries is crucial to its continued success.

Because of this, it is highly recommended that Organization A invest in training its employees, both at the home office and at the field agencies, to better communicate interculturally. In order to help facilitate this, the author of this study will prepare a brief guidebook on intercultural communication for use by Organization A's personnel (see Appendix C).

The results of the research performed in Phase 3 of this study are highly confirmatory of the research performed by other investigators, affirming that cultural approaches and paradigms identified by the likes of Hall, Hofstede, Trompenaars and

Hampden-Turner are accurate and applicable to the specific work team at Organization A. However, the author of this study strongly suggests further research in the area. One possible avenue for future study would be to refine and perfect the validity of the survey instrument (Appendices A and B) in hopes of yielding more meaningful data. Yet another area for future research might involve seeking to determine the extent to which sub-groups or sub-cultures affect one's sensitivity to national culture; in other words, how religion, political affiliation or other subcultures affect conformity to national cultural stereotypes. Finally, Organization A could conduct longitudinal studies when new communications coordinators join its team to compare writing styles to see if they change over time; that is, to observe whether a person from a collectivist culture becomes more individualistic in style the longer he or she is exposed to the mainstream company culture.

References

Adler, N. S. (1997). *International dimensions of organizational behavior.* Cincinnati: South-Western College Publishing.

Ahmed, T., Mouratidis, H., & Preston, D. (2009). Website design guidelines: High power distance and high-context culture. *International Journal of Cyber Society and Education, 2*(1), 47-60. Retrieved August 15, 2011, from http://www.academic-journals.org/ojs2/index.php/IJCSE/article/viewFile/531/16

Analyze a 2x2 contingency table. (2005). Retrieved August 19, 2011, from http://www.graphpad.com/quickcalcs/contingency2.cfm

Bandura, A. (2007). *Everett M. Rogers award colloquium 2007* [video]. Retrieved September 17, 2011, from http://www.youtube.com/watch?v=xjIbKaSXM3A

Basabe, N., & Ros, M. (2005). Cultural dimensions and social behavior correlates: individualism-collectivism and power distance. *Revue Internationale de Psychologie Sociale, 18*(1), 189-225.

Retrieved August 6, 2011, from
http://www.ehu.es/pswparod/pdf/articulos/B
asabe1801.pdf

Bennett, M. (1998). *Intercultural communication: A current perspective*. Retrieved April 23, 2011, from http://www.mairstudents.info/intercultural_c ommunication.pdf

Bos, N., Shami, N., Olson, J., Cheshin, A., & Nan, N. (2004). In-group/out-group effects in distributed teams: An experimental simulation. *Proceedings of the CSCW Chicago 2004*. Chicago, IL: CSCW'04. Retrieved August 8, 2011, from http://tx.technion.ac.il/~acheshin/CSCW04.p df

Campbell, N. (2008). You've got mail! Using email technology to enhance intercultural communication learning. *Journal of Intercultural Communication*, (16). Retrieved May 12, 2011, from http://www.immi.se/intercultural/

Chang, Y. (2011). You think I am stupid? Face needs in intercultural conflicts. *Journal of Intercultural Communication*, (25). Retrieved May 10, 2011, from http://www.immi.se/intercultural/

Chui, K. (2011). Conceptual metaphors in gesture. *Cognitive Linguistics*, *22*(3), 437-458.

Retrieved August 3, 2011, from http://find.galegroup.com/itx/infomark.do?c ontentSet=IAC-Documents&docType=IAC&tabID=T002& prodId=GLRC&docId=A260791643&searc hType=AdvancedSearchForm&type=retriev e&version=1.0

Communication. (2001). In *World of Sociology, Gale*. Retrieved August 3, 2011, from http://ezp.lirn.net/form?qurl=http%3A%2F %2Fwww.credoreference.com/entry/worlds ocs/communication

Francesco, A., & Chen, Z. (2000). *"Cross-cultural" differences within a single culture: Power distance as a moderator of the participation - outcome relationship in the People's Republic of China*. Informally published manuscript, School of Business, Hong Kong Baptist University, Kowloon Tong, Hong Kong. Retrieved August 15, 2011, from http://net2.hkbu.edu.hk/~brc/CCMP200007. pdf

Frith, K. (1994). Consumption and communication: An overview of consumer issues in ASEAN. *Asia Pacific Advances in Consumer Research, 1*, 192-195. Retrieved August 13, 2011, from http://www.acrwebsite.org/volumes/display. asp?id=11208

Gudykunst, W. (1997). Cultural variability in communication. *Communication Research, 24*(4), retrieved April 23, 2011, from http://lirnproxy.museglobal.com/MuseSessio nID=a01ec614ff296870a06bbbb17727d67e/ MuseHost=web1.infotrac-custom.com/MusePath/pdfserve/get_item/1/ A73386435530.pdf

Gudykunst, W. (2005). *Theorizing about intercultural communication.* Thousand Oaks, CA: Sage Publications, Inc.

Hall, E. (1959, 1973). *The silent language.* Garden City, NY: Anchor Press/Doubleday

Hall, E. (1976, 1981). *Beyond culture.* New York, NY: Anchor Books/Doubleday

Hall, E. (1983). *The dance of life.* New York, NY: Anchor Books/Doubleday

Hall, E., & Hall, M. (1990). *Understanding cultural differences.* Yarmouth, ME: Intercultural Press, Inc.

Ho, D., Fu, W., & Ng, S. (2004). Guilt, shame and embarrassment: Revelations of face and self. *Culture & Psychology, 10*(1: 64-84), retrieved August 8, 2011, from http://www.humiliationstudies.org/document s/HoGuiltShameEmbarrassment.pdf doi: DOI: 10.1177/1354067X04044166

Hofstede, G. (1980). *Culture's consequences: International differences in work-related values*. Beverly Hills, CA: Sage Publications.

Hofstede, G. (2009). *Geert Hofstede cultural dimensions*. Retrieved August 6, 2011, from http://www.geert-hofstede.com/

Holliday, Adrian. (2010). Complexity in cultural identity. *Language and Intercultural Communication, 10*(2), retrieved April 23, 2011, from https://www.informaworld.com/smpp/sectio n?content=a922302538&fulltext=71324092 8 doi: 10.1080/14708470903267384

Interpersonal Communication. (2004). In *the Concise Corsini Encyclopedia of Psychology and Behavioral Science*. Retrieved August 3, 2011, from http://ezp.lirn.net/form?qurl=http%3A%2F %2Fwww.credoreference.com/entry/wileyps ych/interpersonal_communication

Jameson, D. (2007, July). Reconceptualizing cultural identity and its role in intercultural business communication. *Journal of Business Communication, 44*(3). Retrieved April 23, 2011, from http://www.niasd.org/pdf/Jameson.pdf doi: 10.1177/0021943607301346

Kaufman-Scarborough, C., & Lindquist, J. (1999). Time management and polychronicity:

Comparisons, contrasts, and insights for the workplace. *Journal of Managerial Psychology, special issue on Polychronicity, 14*(3/4), 288-312. Retrieved August 14, 2011, from http://crab.rutgers.edu/~ckaufman/polychronic.html

Koch, B., & Koch, P. (2007). Collectivism, individualism, and outgroup cooperation in a segmented china. *Asia Pacific Journal of Management, 24*(2), 207-225. Retrieved August 6, 2011, from http://ideas.repec.org/a/kap/asiapa/v24y2007i2p207-225.html

Martin, J., Hammer, M., & Bradford, L. (1994). The influence of cultural and situational contexts on Hispanic and non-Hispanic communication competence behaviors. *Communication Quarterly, 42*(2), retrieved April 23, 2011, from http://proquest.umi.com/pqdweb?index=1&did=4579770&SrchMode=1&sid=3&Fmt=3&VInst=PROD&VType=PQD&RQT=309&VName=PQD&TS=1303452443&clientId=83181

McFarlin, D., & Sweeney, P. (2006). *International management: Strategic opportunities and cultural challenges.* Boston, MA: Houghton Mifflin Company

Murphy, M., & Levy, M. (2006). Politeness in intercultural email communication: Australian and Korean perspectives. *Journal of Business Communication*, (12). Retrieved May 12, 2011, from http://www.immi.se/intercultural/ ISSN 1404-1634

Nordby, H. (2008). Values, cultural identity and communication: A perspective from philosophy of language. *Journal of Intercultural Communication*, (17). Retrieved April 23, 2011, from http://www.immi.se/intercultural/nr17/nordby.htm

Olk, H. (2009). Translation, cultural knowledge and intercultural competence. *Journal of Intercultural Communication*, (20). Retrieved May 10, 2011, from http://www.immi.se/intercultural/

Rosenberg, S. (2004, February). *Face*. Retrieved August 8, 2011, from http://crinfo.beyondintractability.org/c101/28787.jsp

Samovar, L., Porter, R., & McDaniel, E. (2009). *Communication between cultures*. Boston, MA: Wadsworth. Retrieved August 13, 2011, from http://books.google.com/books?id=fxmSZD9gftkC&pg=PA290&lpg=PA290&dq=harm

ony+and+communication+culture&source=
bl&ots=_utkbaxiyr&sig=KmOo0GydR5t5hf
QAGUzBVgq9HjM&hl=en&ei=74NGToz_
J-uOsAK-
sqiSCA&sa=X&oi=book_result&ct=result&
resnum=4&ved=0CC8Q6AEwAzgU#v=one
page&q=harmony%20and%20communicati
on%20culture&f=false

Samovar, L., Porter, R., & McDaniel, E. (2010). *Intercultural communication: A reader.* Boston, MA: Wadsworth.

Schmader, T., & Major, B. (1998). The impact of ingroup vs outgroup performance on personal values. *Journal of Experimental Social Psychology, 35,* 47-67. Retrieved August 6, 2011, from http://www.ncsu.edu/odi/advance/document s/Theimpactofingroupvs.outgroup.pdf

Scribner, S., & Cole, M. (1978). Literacy without schooling: Testing for intellectual effects. *Harvard Educational Review, 48*(4), 448-461. Retrieved September 17, 2011, from http://www.utpa.edu/dept/curr_ins/faculty_f olders/Guadarrama_i/literacy/Scribner_Cole .pdf

Seo, K., Miller, P., Schmidt, C., & Sowa, P. (2008). A comparison of online communication patterns between Hong Kong and U.S. students. *Journal of Intercultural*

Communication, (18). Retrieved May 11, 2011, from http://www.immi.se/intercultural/

Shi, Y., & Fan, S. (2010). An analysis of non-verbal behaviour in intercultural communication. *The International Journal of Language, Society and Culture*, (31), retrieved August 1, 2011, from http://www.educ.utas.edu.au/users/tle/JOUR NAL/issues/2010/31-14.pdf

Sørnes, J., Stephens, K., Sætre, A., & Browning, L. (2004). The reflexivity between ICTs and business culture: Applying Hofstede's theory to compare Norway and the United States. *Informing Science Journal*, 7, 1-30. Retrieved August 13, 2011, from http://inform.nu/Articles/Vol7/v7p001-030-211.pdf.

Storti, C. (1994). *Cross-cultural dialogues: 74 brief encounters with cultural difference*. Boston, MA: Intercultural Press

Tran, D., & Skitmore, M. (2002). The impact of culture on international management: a survey of project communications in Singapore. *The Australian Journal of Construction Economics and Building*, 2(2), 36-47. Retrieved August 11, 2011, from http://eprints.qut.edu.au/3440/1/3440_1.pdf

Trompenaars, F., & Hampden-Turner, C. (1998). *Riding the waves of culture: Understanding diversity in global business.* New York, NY: McGraw-Hill

Tuleja, E., & O'Rourke, J. (2009). *Intercultural communication for business.* Mason, OH: South Western Cengage Learning

Wei, W., Yuen, E., & Zhu, J. (2001). *Individualism-collectivism and conflict resolution styles: a cross-cultural study of managers in Singapore.* Unpublished manuscript, Department of Management & Organization, Faculty of Business Administration, National University of Singapore, Singapore. Retrieved May 11, 2011, from http://www.justice.gov/adr/events/Materials. Nov19.0106.pdf

World map of masculinity - Hofstede. (2011). Retrieved August 13, 2011, from http://www.kwintessential.co.uk/map/hofste de-masculinity.html

Yi, J. (2002). Individualism-collectivism: A study of college students in four countries. *Journal of the Speech and Theatre Association of Missouri, 32.* Retrieved August 6, 2011, from http://www.stamnet.org/journal/volume32/ju ngsooyi.pdf

Yuan, W. (2009). Effectiveness of communication between American and Chinese employees in multinational organizations in China. *Intercultural Communication Studies, 18*(1), 188-204.

Appendix A

Communications Survey Instrument

Groups A and B

Name:
Date:
Country:

Instructions:

Thank you for participating in this survey. Your answers will help us improve our communications between Organization A and our SOAs in each country where we work.

Your participation in this survey, though very important, is completely voluntary. It is part of a research project that is being conducted by Kelly Nix and is not officially sponsored by Organization A, although it is hoped that Organization A will benefit significantly from the findings.

When answering the survey questions, please observe the following:

- Please answer **ALL** the questions. Leaving a check box blank will affect the accuracy of the survey results. Even if a response is not exactly what you would think or feel, choose

the option that is **closest** to the way you think you would react.
- Be completely honest in your answers; <u>there are no right or wrong answers</u>, and your honest response will be extremely important in maintaining the accuracy of the conclusions of this research.
- Your responses will in no way affect our perception of you as an employee, nor will they be considered in your performance evaluation.
- Please do not try to guess which are the answers we expect. You might be surprised!
- Do not overthink your answers. We are more interested in your initial reactions than we are a reasoned response.

Please send the completed survey to Kelly Nix at knix@organizationa.org immediately upon completing it.

Thanks again for your participation!

Kelly Nix

Question 1

You receive the following message in an email from the content manager at Organization A to all communications coordinators:

"We are concerned because lately we have noticed a marked increase in the number of story ideas and follow-ups that are being submitted late. Please remember that it is critical that you submit your material on time. Late submissions cannot be tolerated."

Assume you **are** one of the communications coordinators that have been submitting work late. Which of the following reactions to the above message are you *most likely* to have?

   A. "I need to work on getting my assignments in on time. If I don't, I may be reprimanded."
   B. "It seems a lot of us are having the same problem. My fellow communications coordinators and I should talk about the problem and see what we can do to fix it."

Answer (check one):   A ☐   B ☐

Please briefly explain why you selected this answer:

Question 2

You receive the following message in an email from the content manager at Organization A to all communications coordinators:

"We are concerned because lately we have noticed a marked increase in the number of story ideas and follow-ups that are being submitted late. Please remember that it is critical that you submit your material on time. Late submissions cannot be tolerated."

Assume you are **not** one of the communications coordinators that have been submitting work late. Which of the following reactions to the above message are you *most likely* to have?

    A. You email back immediately to remind the content manager that you are usually, if not always, punctual with your assignments.

    B. You say nothing, because you realize that although you are punctual, others on the team may not always be; therefore, it seems reasonable that the entire team should be admonished.

Answer (check one):   A ☐   B ☐

Please briefly explain why you selected this answer:

Question 3

You receive the following message in an email from the content manager at Organization A to all communications coordinators:

"Yesterday was the deadline for XYZ project. Thanks to all of you who submitted your assignments. So far, we have only received submissions from the following agencies: ABC, DEF and GHI."

Assume you **are** the communications coordinator from agency ABC. Which reaction are you *most likely* to have?

A. "It makes me feel good that my hard work on this assignment is recognized. I'm glad the email mentions that I have already submitted; I would hate for anyone to think I was late."

B. "Wow...I wish the email hadn't mentioned me specifically. The other communications coordinators who are late must feel terrible."

Answer (check one):   A ☐   B ☐

Please briefly explain why you selected this answer:

Question 4

You receive the following message in an email from the content manager at Organization A to all communications coordinators:

"Yesterday was the deadline for XYZ project. Thanks to all of you who submitted your assignments. So far, we have only received submissions from the following agencies: ABC, DEF and GHI."

Assume you **are** the communications coordinator from one of the agencies that has *not yet submitted*. Which reaction are you *most likely* to have?

- A. "I feel humiliated. This email has embarrassed me in front of all my colleagues."
- B. "It's only fair that those who met the deadline be named. After all, they worked hard to get their work in on time, so it would not be fair for them to be reprimanded along with everyone else."

Answer (check one):   A ☐   B ☐

Please briefly explain why you selected this answer:

Question 5

You receive the following message in an email from the content manager at Organization A to all communications coordinators:

"Yesterday was the deadline for XYZ project. Thanks to all of you who submitted your assignments. So far, we have only received submissions from the following agencies: ABC, DEF and GHI."

The email is copied to all agency directors.

Assume you **are** the communications coordinator from agency ABC. Which reaction are you **most likely** to have?

    A. "I'm glad they mentioned that I turned my work in on time. I feel sorry for the other communications coordinators, but it's important for my boss to know I'm doing my job."
    B. "Wow...I wish the email hadn't mentioned me specifically. I hope this doesn't cause the other communications coordinators to feel badly toward me."

Answer (check one): A ☐ B ☐

Please briefly explain why you selected this answer:

Question 6

You receive the following message in an email from the content manager at Organization A to all communications coordinators:

"Yesterday was the deadline for XYZ project. Thanks to all of you who submitted your assignments. So far, we have only received submissions from the following agencies: ABC, DEF and GHI."

The email is copied to all agency directors.

Assume you **are** the communications coordinator from one of the agencies that has *not yet submitted*. Which reaction are you *most likely* to have?

    A. "I'm really not concerned about my boss seeing that I haven't submitted this project yet. If he/she asks me about it, I'll explain how busy I've been with other critical projects, and he/she will understand."
    B. "I wish the email would have been more general, and I wish our bosses hadn't been copied. I'm afraid this will hurt my agency director's confidence in me, even though I have been buried in critical projects."

Answer (check one):   A ☐   B ☐

Please briefly explain why you selected this answer:

Question 7

You receive the following message in an email from the content manager at Organization A to all communications coordinators:

"This is just a reminder that the deadline for project XYZ is approaching. Please be certain that all materials for the project are submitted on or before the due date."

As a communications coordinator receiving this email, which reaction are you *most likely* to have?

A. "Deadlines are important, but many other factors come into play in carrying out a project. I will turn in the project as close to the deadline as possible, but it's only reasonable to understand that circumstances in the field may cause it to be a day or two late."

B. "This project must be turned in exactly by the due date. Being on time is so important that I will work extra hours in the evenings and on weekends if necessary to meet the deadline."

Answer (check one):   A ☐   B ☐

Please briefly explain why you selected this answer:

Question 8

You receive the following message in an email from the content manager at Organization A to all communications coordinators:

"Project XYZ is extremely critical and takes top priority over any other projects you are working on. If you have other projects that are in conflict with this project, please let me know and I will be happy to contact your agency director to help reprioritize your assignments."

As a communications coordinator receiving this email, which reaction are you *most likely* to have?

    A. "It would be very helpful for the Organization A content manager to contact my agency director to explain why this project is more important than anything else I am working on."

    B. "I would prefer to reprioritize my assignments myself, even if it means working overtime to complete all my projects. When I receive special intervention from the home office, it makes my coworkers at the agency feel resentful toward me."

Answer (check one):   A ☐   B ☐

Please briefly explain why you selected this answer:

Appendix B
Communications Survey Instrument
Groups C and D

Name:
Date:

Instructions:

Thank you for participating in this survey. Your answers will help us better understand how an individual's national culture affects his or her understanding and perception of business communications.

Your participation in this survey, though very important, is completely voluntary. It is part of a research project that is being conducted by Kelly Nix. It is our hope that the information gained from this project will be of special benefit to the work of foreign missions.

When answering the survey questions, please observe the following important instructions:

- Please answer **ALL** the questions. Leaving a check box blank will affect the accuracy of the survey results. Even if a response is not exactly what you would think or feel, choose

the option that is **closest** to the way you think you would react.
- Be completely honest in your answers; there are no right or wrong answers, and your honest response will be extremely important in maintaining the accuracy of the conclusions of this research.
- Please do not try to guess which are the answers we expect. You might be surprised!
- Do not overthink your answers. We are more interested in your initial reactions than we are a reasoned response.

Please send the completed survey to Kelly Nix at knbrazil@email.com immediately upon completing it.

Thanks again for your participation!

Kelly Nix

Setting

For purposes of this survey, please imagine you are a minister associated with a ministerial organization. As such, you operate under a local supervisor (referred to in this document as a "presbyter"), who in turn answers to a regional supervisor. You work very closely with your organization and receive task assignments directly from it.

As part of your ministerial responsibilities, each month you are expected to turn in an activity report for your local congregation. The following survey questions will be based on this scenario.

Question 1

You receive the following message in an email from the regional director to all ministers:

"We are concerned because lately we have noticed a marked increase in the number of monthly reports that are being submitted late. Please remember that it is critical that you submit your material on time. Late submissions cannot be tolerated."

Assume you **are** one of the ministers that have been submitting reports late. Which of the following reactions to the above message are you *most likely* to have?

    C. "I need to work on getting my reports in on time. If I don't, I may be reprimanded."

    D. "It seems a lot of us are having the same problem. My fellow ministers and I should talk about the problem and see what we can do to fix it."

Answer (check one):   A ☐   B ☐

Please briefly explain why you selected this answer:

Question 2

You receive the following message in an email from the regional director to all ministers:

"We are concerned because lately we have noticed a marked increase in the number of monthly reports that are being submitted late. Please remember that it is critical that you submit your material on time. Late submissions cannot be tolerated."

Assume you are **not** one of the ministers that have been submitting reports late. Which of the following reactions to the above message are you *most likely* to have?

C. You email back immediately to remind the regional director that you are usually, if not always, punctual with your reports.

D. You say nothing, because you realize that although you are punctual, other ministers in your region may not always be; therefore, it seems reasonable that the entire team should be admonished.

Answer (check one):   A ☐   B ☐

Please briefly explain why you selected this answer:

Question 3

You receive the following message in an email from the regional director to all ministers:

"Yesterday was the deadline for the monthly report. Thanks to all of you who submitted your reports. So far, we have only received reports from the following ministers: John Doe, Jim Doe and Billy Doe."

Assume you **are** one of the ministers listed above. Which reaction are you *most likely* to have?

C. "It makes me feel good that my hard work on this report is recognized. I'm glad the email mentions that I have already submitted; I would hate for anyone to think I was late."

D. "Wow...I wish the email hadn't mentioned me specifically. The other ministers who are late must feel terrible."

Answer (check one):   A ☐   B ☐

Please briefly explain why you selected this answer:

Question 4

You receive the following message in an email from the regional director to all ministers:

"Yesterday was the deadline for the monthly report. Thanks to all of you who submitted your reports. So far, we have only received reports from the following ministers: John Doe, Jim Doe and Billy Doe."

Assume you **are** one of the ministers that has **not yet submitted**. Which reaction are you **most likely** to have?

C. "I feel humiliated. This email has embarrassed me in front of all my fellow ministers."

D. "It's only fair that those who met the deadline be named. After all, they worked hard to get their work in on time, so it would not be fair for them to be reprimanded along with everyone else."

Answer (check one): A ☐ B ☐

Please briefly explain why you selected this answer:

Question 5

You receive the following message in an email from the regional director to all ministers:

"Yesterday was the deadline for the monthly report. Thanks to all of you who submitted your reports. So far, we have only received reports from the following ministers: John Doe, Jim Doe and Billy Doe."

The email is copied to all presbyters.

Assume you **are** one of the ministers listed above. Which reaction are you *most likely* to have?

    C. "I'm glad they mentioned that I turned my work in on time. I feel sorry for the other ministers, but it's important for my boss to know I'm doing my job."

    D. "Wow...I wish the email hadn't mentioned me specifically. I hope this doesn't cause the other ministers to feel badly toward me."

Answer (check one):   A ☐   B ☐

Please briefly explain why you selected this answer:

Question 6

You receive the following message in an email from the regional director to all ministers:

"Yesterday was the deadline for the monthly report. Thanks to all of you who submitted your reports. So far, we have only received reports from the following ministers: John Doe, Jim Doe and Billy Doe."

The email is copied to all presbyters.

Assume you **are** one of the ministers that has *not yet submitted*. Which reaction are you *most likely* to have?

C. "I'm really not concerned about my boss seeing that I haven't submitted this report yet. If he asks me about it, I'll explain how busy I've been with other critical projects, and he will understand."

D. "I wish the email would have been more general, and I wish our bosses hadn't been copied. I'm afraid this will hurt my presbyter's confidence in me, even though I have been buried in critical projects."

Answer (check one):　A ☐　　B ☐

Please briefly explain why you selected this answer:

Question 7

You receive the following message in an email from the regional director to all ministers:

"This is just a reminder that the deadline for the monthly report is approaching. Please be certain that all materials for the report are submitted on or before the due date."

As a communications coordinator receiving this email, which reaction are you *most likely* to have?

    C. "Deadlines are important, but many other factors come into play in carrying out a project. I will turn in the report as close to the deadline as possible, but it's only reasonable to understand that circumstances at my church may cause it to be a day or two late."

    D. "This project must be turned in exactly by the due date. Being on time is so important that I will work extra hours in the evenings and on weekends if necessary to meet the deadline."

Answer (check one):   A ☐   B ☐

Please briefly explain why you selected this answer:

Question 8

You receive the following message in an email from the regional director to all ministers:

"The monthly report is extremely critical and takes top priority over any other projects you are working on. If you have other projects that are in conflict with this report, please let me know and I will be happy to contact your presbyter to help reprioritize your assignments."

As a minister receiving this email, which reaction are you *most likely* to have?

C. "It would be very helpful for the regional director to contact my presbyter to explain why this report is more important than anything else I am working on."

D. "I would prefer to reprioritize my assignments myself, even if it means working overtime to complete all my projects. When I receive special intervention from the regional director, it makes my fellow ministers feel resentful toward me."

Answer (check one):   A ☐   B ☐

Please briefly explain why you selected this answer:

Appendix C
Intercultural Communication Guidebook:

A Handbook for Employees of Organization A

By Kelly Nix

Communication is simple, right? I say it, you hear it and you understand it. What could be difficult about that?

Lots.

In 1949, a couple of researchers by the name of Shannon and Weaver came up with the following model:[1]

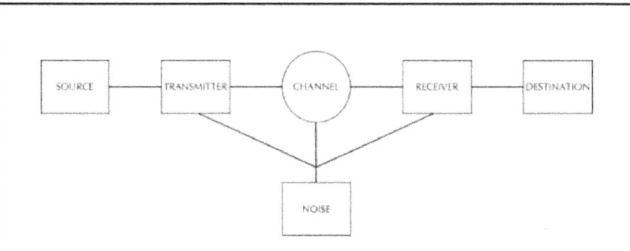

Figure 1.1. A model depicting the mechanics of human communications. Adapted from "Intercultural Communication," 2004, *The Concise Corsini Encyclopedia of Psychology and Behavioral Science.*

It doesn't take a rocket scientist to look at this chart and realize there is a lot more to true communication than just having one person say

[1] Adapted from "Intercultural Communication," 2004, *The Concise Corsini Encyclopedia of Psychology and Behavioral Science.*

something and another person hear it. You have to consider the *channel* through which the message is being communicated. And most importantly, you have to consider the noise – think static on a radio channel – or interference the message has to go through before the receiver can decode it – assuming the receiver is on the same channel as the sender. And what if the receiver doesn't think like the sender in the first place?

In other words, there are plenty of ways for communication to go wrong. While this document can't begin to address all of them, it will cover some of the most common issues. Hopefully, what is covered here will be at least a tiny step in the direction of improving communication within our organization – particularly among individuals from different national cultures.

Defining communication

For starters, we should probably explain exactly what we mean by "communication." Of course, if we are actually successful in doing this, we'll be doing better than dozens – perhaps hundreds – of researchers have done so far! Everybody seems to have a little different take on what communication means – which might explain why it's so difficult to communicate effectively in the first place.

For the sake of simplicity, we'll use one from an article in *World of Sociology* that says that communication is "the conveyance of information, including such things as thoughts and messages, and takes place using visual signs and sounds such as language."[2] But to further complicate things, many of the people with whom we communicate within the organization are not located in the home office. Instead, they reside in entirely different countries and speak entirely different languages. They can't even *see* us, which is a real problem...because, in the words of one researcher, "metaphoric gestures can provide salient, additional information about the aspect of the conceptualization which is the speaker's focus of attention in real-time multimodal communication."[3]

Or, to put that in English, the gestures you make with your hands and the expressions on your face

[2] Communication. (2001). In *World of Sociology, Gale.* Retrieved August 3, 2011, from http://ezp.lirn.net/form?qurl=http%3A%2F%2Fwww.credoref erence.com/entry/worldsocs/communication

[3] Chui, K. (2011). Conceptual metaphors in gesture. *Cognitive Linguistics, 22*(3), 437-458. Retrieved August 3, 2011, from http://find.galegroup.com/itx/infomark.do?contentSet=IAC-Documents&docType=IAC&tabID=T002&prodId=GLRC&d ocId=A260791643&searchType=AdvancedSearchForm&type =retrieve&version=1.0

can really help your hearers understand what you're saying.

Edward Hall, the granddaddy of intercultural communication research, understood the challenges that can be created when you take the already difficult task of communicating and mix it with the additional challenge of making that communication understandable to someone from another culture that may think in a way that is entirely different from the way your culture thinks. That's why he pointed out the importance of "an introduction to the non-verbal language which exists in every country of the world and among the various groups within each country."[4] Of course, communication by email doesn't help much with non-verbal language, does it? That means we have to try even *harder* to make ourselves clearly understood when communicating by electronic means.

So what is "culture"?

We've talked a lot about communication, and we've referred to "intercultural" communication...so what exactly does culture mean?

---

[4] Hall, E. (1959, 1973). *The silent language.* Garden City, NY: Anchor Press/Doubleday

That's another one of those really good questions. Just as "communication" has several meanings, so does "culture."

Edward Hall defined culture as "the way of life of a people," and the "sum of their learned behavior patterns, attitudes, and material things."[5] He goes on to argue that culture is a series of situational models for behavior and thought, and that it affects personality, the way people express themselves and show emotion, the way they think, the way they move, the way they solve problems, how they build their cities, how they plan their transportation systems, and how they put together their economic and government systems.

Fons Trompenaars and his research partner, Charles Hampden-Turner, echo the conclusion of a guy named Schein (1985) who proposed that culture is "the way in which a group of people solves problems and reconciles dilemmas.[6] They believe that culture comes in layers that must be peeled back to allow observation, revealing deeper

---

[5] Hall, E. (1976, 1981). *Beyond culture*. New York, NY: Anchor Books/Doubleday

[6] Trompenaars, F., & Hampden-Turner, C. (1998). *Riding the waves of culture: Understanding diversity in global business.* New York, NY: McGraw-Hill.

values and norms in a society that are not directly visible. These values affect how people approach their relationships with other people, the passage of time and the environment.

Then you have McFarlin and Sweeney, who agree with Hofstede's (1993) view that culture is "the collective programming of the mind which distinguishes one group or category of people from another. They further agree that this cultural programming is not directly observable but can only be inferred from behavior, and that people are "often unaware of the pervasive impact of culture on their own attitudes, beliefs and behaviors." But they also caution that culture is a concept that is only useful if it can accurately predict behavior, and that many cultural groups can coexist within different countries.[7]

This isn't getting any easier, is it?

Culture and communication

It would be nice if we could ignore the whole culture issue and just write. But if we do so, we run

---

[7] McFarlin, D., & Sweeney, P. (2006). *International management: Strategic opportunities and cultural challenges.* Boston, MA: Houghton Mifflin Company.

the risk of our readers completely missing our message. Shi and Fan use research by Arasaratnam & Banerjee (2007) and Ma (1996) as evidence that failures or misunderstandings in intercultural communication are largely caused by the misinterpretation or misuse of nonverbal behaviors. They also refer to the findings of Lustig & Koester (2006) that "miscommunication always occurred in the understanding of nonverbal behaviors because different social contexts might create extremely different rules for appropriate and effective use of nonverbal behaviors."[8]

That makes our job as remote communicators all that much tougher. Non-verbal behavior is critical to effective communication, and we don't get the benefit of using it. We're starting out at a disadvantage!

Cultural aspects

If you do much research at all in the area of intercultural communication, you'll come across the term "cultural aspects" in reference to things

---

[8] Shi, Y., & Fan, S. (2010). An analysis of non-verbal behaviour in intercultural communication. *The International Journal of Language, Society and Culture*, (31), retrieved August 1, 2011, from http://www.educ.utas.edu.au/users/tle/JOURNAL/issues/2010/31-14.pdf

that can cause "static" when we try to communicate across cultures. Hofstede has been one of the primary definers of cultural aspects, and others have chimed in as well. Some of the primary cultural aspects to be considered include individualism/collectivism, context, face, uncertainty avoidance, harmony, and concepts of time. Let's take a brief look at what these mean. But before we do, let's just reinforce one thing: these aspects are *generalizations*. Acknowledging that certain cultures tend toward these aspects does not mean that *every single person* in those cultures thinks this way; it's just how *most people* within a culture tend to think.

Individualism/collectivism. This aspect has nothing to do with politics. Instead, it simply refers to whether a person operates more as a lone wolf or as a member of the pack. Hofstede defines individualism – and consequently its opposite, collectivism – as "the degree to which individuals are integrated into groups." Individualist societies are characterized by loose ties between individuals, with each person responsible for looking out for him- or herself and the immediate family unit. Conversely, Hofstede holds that people in collectivist societies are conditioned from their birth to integrate into strong, cohesive in-groups that continue protecting them in exchange for unquestioning loyalty.[9]

Here are some interesting considerations from Trompenaars and Hampden-Turner. They assert that communitarian cultures prefer plural representation in negotiations, while individualistic cultures have high esteem for the concept of a single representative voting his or her private conscience on behalf of the representative's constituents. People of influence in individualistic cultures may be lone operators, but in communitarian cultures unaccompanied people are assumed to lack status. Anglo-Saxons expect translators in business negotiations to remain neutral, while communitarian cultures expect the translator to serve the national group as a mediator of misunderstandings that arise from culture and language.[10]

---

[9] Hofstede, G. (2009). *Geert Hofstede cultural dimensions*. Retrieved August 6, 2011, from http://www.geert-hofstede.com/

[10] Trompenaars, F., & Hampden-Turner, C. (1998). *Riding the waves of culture: Understanding diversity in global business*. New York, NY: McGraw-Hill.

But there are even more differences! Communitarian-based decision making is typically lengthy and consultative, seeking to achieve consensus, while individualistic decision-makers may simply vote down the dissenters. Additionally, the two dimensions are often motivated by different things; individualists tend to strive for "individually resplendent self-actualization at the summit of the hierarchy," while communitarians may be more motivated by the idea of the positive regard and support of their colleagues. Finally, there are different perceptions of organizational structure; to the individualist, organizations tend to be viewed as instruments that have been deliberately assembled in order to serve individual owners, employees and customers, while the communitarian may view the organization as a social context that is shared by all members and which gives them meaning and purpose, serves as a family that develops and nurtures its members, and may in fact outlive them.[11]

Now consider the fact that our organization's home office is based in the United States, a highly individualistic society. But all – or practically all – of our field agencies are located in countries that are

[11] Ibid.

strongly collectivist in culture.[12] Can you see where that could pose a problem to communication?

Context. This just might be the absolutely most important aspect of cultural variability when it comes to how we communicate as an organization.

We'll let Dr. Hall explain context to us. He says that in high context cultures people are deeply involved with each other, information is widely shared and simple messages with deep meanings flow freely. He observes that high context cultures are "likely to be overwhelmed by mechanical systems and lose their integrity" – an observation that seems less likely to be completely accurate in today's technology-infused society than it would have been at the time of Hall's writing, yet nevertheless may hold true in a broader sense. In low context cultures, on the other hand, people are highly individualized and have relatively little involvement with other people. Messages must be much more detailed in low context cultures, because less of the meaning of the communication can be derived from the environment.[13]

---

[12] Ibid.

[13] Hall, E. (1976, 1981). *Beyond culture.* New York, NY: Anchor Books/Doubleday

Hall says that "the level of context determines everything about the nature of the communication and is the foundation on which all subsequent behavior rests." The importance of this becomes clear when you realize that individuals from high context cultures are less likely to communicate their needs or frustrations directly and will "talk around" the subject because they expect the hearer to understand what is bothering them. This is because stating the conclusion for the listener is tantamount to an insult and a violation of his or her individuality.[14] This tendency, of course, can be quite frustrating to listeners from low context societies such as the United States, who often become irritated at speakers from other cultures for "beating around the bush."

Hall also points out that "high-context cultures make greater distinction between insiders and outsiders than low-context cultures do."[15] This is really important. This is known as "ingroup bias." Imagine the effect that can be produced when a member of the local field agency team appears to be receiving special attention from the home office

---

[14] Ibid.

[15] Ibid.

that is not given to other members of the field agency team, or the ingroup....

High-context cultures tend to be communitarian, and low-context cultures tend to be individualistic. So, unfortunately, the United States is low-context and our field agencies are high-context – yet another hurdle for effective intraorganizational communication.

Hall sums our problem up like this: he says that that "if the LC [low context] person interacting with a high-context culture does not really think things through and try to foresee all contingencies, he's headed for trouble."[16] Well said, Dr. Hall!

Face. This is much more than just the thing that hangs on the front of your head. In fact, it's a vitally important aspect of intercultural communication. If you make somebody lose it, your proverbial goose is cooked.

Craig Storti says that "face" is "the image one presents to the world, including one's reputation." He argues that face is "closely linked to the notion of self-esteem or self-worth...and if at all possible one does not want to lose one's face, especially in

---

[16] Ibid.

public."[17] Other researchers have defined loss of face as "a damaging social event, in which one's action is publicly given notice and negatively judged by others, resulting in a loss of moral or social standing."[18]

Managing face in communications is critical. Gudykunst cites the assertion by Cupach & Imahori (1993) that "the ability to maintain face in interactions is one indicator of individuals' interpersonal communication competence," and that "intercultural communication competence involves successfully managing face...."[19]

Is this important to what we do? Consider that we have agencies in Asia, and McFarlin & Sweeney observe, based on the work of Reeder (1987), that the need for face (the regard of others) may be the single most important concept to be aware of in

---

[17] Storti, C. (1994). *Cross-cultural dialogues: 74 brief encounters with cultural difference.* Boston, MA: Intercultural Press

[18] Ho, D., Fu, W., & Ng, S. (2004). Guilt, shame and embarrassment: Revelations of face and self. *Culture & Psychology, 10*(1: 64-84), retrieved August 8, 2011, from http://www.humiliationstudies.org/documents/HoGuiltShame Embarrassment.pdf doi: DOI: 10.1177/1354067X04044166

[19] Gudykunst, W. (2005). *Theorizing about intercultural communication.* Thousand Oaks, CA: Sage Publications, Inc.

many Asian cultures, and that, since many Asian cultures are interdependent, they also try to save face for others. They also point out that, in some cultures, to not know is to lose face. Therefore, an individual may provide information that is inaccurate rather than not provide information at all. Furthermore, because the affording of face is mutual, individuals in these cultures might proceed according to someone's instructions even knowing that the outcome would be undesirable rather than cause the other party to lose face by pointing out that their instructions were flawed. Additionally, some cultures find it difficult to say no, so they communicate this to you in roundabout language that you are expected to understand.[20]

Practical experience indicates face is not just an issue in Asia. It is a consideration worldwide – just to varying degrees.

So the answer is "yes." Face is an issue we must be keenly aware of, particularly when copying an agency director on an email that rebukes or criticizes the work of a communications coordinator. Remember, our agencies exist in

---

[20] McFarlin, D., & Sweeney, P. (2006). *International management: Strategic opportunities and cultural challenges.* Boston, MA: Houghton Mifflin Company.

cultures that are high context. Citing Cohen (1997), Rosenberg (2004) states that high context communication is "primarily concerned with maintaining face and group harmony," and that "every word is considered carefully, and many expressions of respect and courtesy are included" because "being rebuffed could cause loss of face."[21]

Uncertainty avoidance. Hofstede developed an "Uncertainty Avoidance Index (UAI)" to address a society's tolerance for uncertainty and ambiguity, or the extent to which it programs its members to feel either uncomfortable or comfortable in unstructured situations. Cultures that avoid uncertainty attempt to minimize the possibility of unstructured situations and safety and security measures. They also hold to the belief that there is one absolute truth, and that they have it. People in these cultures tend to be more emotional. On the other hand, cultures that accept uncertainty tend to be more tolerant of differing opinions, have fewer rules and are more relativist in areas of philosophy and politics, and their people are more

---

[21] Rosenberg, S. (2004, February). *Face.* Retrieved August 8, 2011, from http://crinfo.beyondintractability.org/c101/28787.jsp

phlegmatic, more contemplative and are not expected to express emotions. High context cultures tend to be uncertainty avoidant, while low context cultures have a greater tolerance for uncertainty.[22]

So there you have it. High context societies are also highly uncertainty-avoidant. We low-context people are not. Change is often not a big a deal to us...but beware. When we are constantly changing priorities or the way we do things, we can make the employees at our agencies very, very uncomfortable. According to Tuleja and O'Rourke, high uncertainty-avoidance cultures attempt to prevent unstructured situations by maximizing predictability through establishing rules and strict codes of behavior, apparently embracing the motto that "what is different is dangerous." They also point out that business characteristics of these cultures may include a lengthier time required to integrate new employees into long-standing workgroups, more dependency on the authority and direction provided by leaders, less tolerance of risk, and more preoccupation with consensus and

---

[22] Hofstede, G. (2009). *Geert Hofstede cultural dimensions.* Retrieved August 6, 2011, from http://www.geert-hofstede.com/

harmony for the good of the greater group than what would be found in less uncertainty-avoidant cultures."[23]

Again...the United States is highly tolerant of uncertainty. The rest of the countries where we work are not. That doesn't make things any easier.

Harmony. In America, we are taught that assertiveness is a desirable virtue. But not every culture sees through the same lens on this issue. In fact, some cultures see assertiveness as "threatening and detrimental to genial interpersonal relationships." Samovar, Porter and McDaniel learned through research that the Filipino culture places particular value on interpersonal harmony, and that the Filipino concept of harmony relates to a "very fragile sense of personal worth and self-respect." They add that Filipinos are especially vulnerable to negative remarks that might affect their standing in society (making the ideas of harmony and face closely related), and that Filipinos rarely criticize or confront others, using extreme politeness when criticism or confrontations are unavoidable.

[23] Tuleja, E., & O'Rourke, J. (2009). *Intercultural communication for business.* Mason, OH: South Western Cengage Learning

Bluntness and frankness are viewed by Filipino society as uncivilized traits.[24]

This outlook is diametrically opposed to American culture, whose "long history of valuing nonconformity, individualism, competition, freedom of expression, and even some select forms of rebellion is bound to encourage assertive behavior." (Samovar, et al, 2009, p. 291). Conversely, the Japanese often are so averse to confrontation that they refuse to say "no," resorting instead to more evasive responses, while the Mexican culture is said to value harmony so much that the concept of truth may become situational – so much so that "in order to sustain positive relations or make the other person feel better, Mexicans may slightly alter the facts or withhold important negative information." [25]

---

[24] Samovar, L., Porter, R., & McDaniel, E. (2009). *Communication between cultures*. Boston, MA: Wadsworth. Retrieved August 13, 2011, from http://books.google.com/books?id=fxmSZD9gftkC&pg=PA29 0&lpg=PA290&dq=harmony+and+communication+culture&s ource=bl&ots=_utkbaxiyr&sig=KmOo0GydR5t5hfQAGUzB Vgq9HjM&hl=en&ei=74NGToz_J-uOsAK-sqiSCA&sa=X&oi=book_result&ct=result&resnum=4&ved= 0CC8Q6AEwAzgU#v=onepage&q=harmony%20and%20com munication%20culture&f=false

[25] Ibid.

Meanwhile, Frith echoes Kincaid's (1987) assertion that the most important aspect of communication in most Asian cultures is the maintenance of social harmony.[26]

Time. This can be the most frustrating cultural aspect for many people to deal with. Edward Hall makes the provocative observation that Anglo Americans "tend to think that because nothing overt is happening, nothing is going on." He divides time into two major perspectives: polychronic and monochronic. In polychronic time, people do many things at once, while in monochronic time people tend to be more linear. High context cultures tend to be polychronic, and low context cultures more monochronic.[27]

Hall divides time into two major perspectives: polychronic and monochronic. In polychronic time, people do many things at once, while in monochronic time people tend to be more linear.

---

[26] Frith, K. (1994). Consumption and communication: An overview of consumer issues in ASEAN. *Asia Pacific Advances in Consumer Research*, *1*, 192-195. Retrieved August 13, 2011, from http://www.acrwebsite.org/volumes/display.asp?id=11208

[27] Hall, E. (1983). *The dance of life*. New York, NY: Anchor Books/Doubleday

High context cultures tend to be polychronic, and low context cultures more monochronic [28] – meaning our organization's home office operates monochronically, while the field agencies are polychronic.

Polychronic cultures have a very different perception of time than do monochronic cultures. In monochronic cultures like the United States, people tend to be dominated by schedules and by the clock. Tasks take precedence over personal relationships. Everything is driven by deadlines. In polychronic cultures, however, people view time as something to be used by them rather than as a lord over them. They value human relations above schedules; therefore, it is only natural to delay a scheduled event if a person of importance to them has a more pressing need.[29]

A very interesting and critically important aspect of the polychronic time orientation is that supervisors in polychronic societies may provide a subordinate with a very detailed list of activities to be completed in order to satisfactorily discharge his or her responsibilities, **but they would never presume**

---

[28] Ibid.

[29] Ibid.

to schedule the execution of those activities, because "for an employer to schedule a subordinate's work for him would be considered a tyrannical violation of his individuality – an invasion of the self." This contrasts with monochronic cultures' tendency to schedule the activity and leave the analysis of the activities of the job to the individual.[30] **This should cause us to use utmost caution in avoiding the American tendency to micromanage projects when dealing with the field agencies.**

In his analysis, Hall acknowledges that both time orientations – monochronic and polychronic – have inherent weaknesses. He points out that polychronic organizations are limited in size, depend on having gifted people at the top and are slow and cumbersome when dealing with anything new or different, creating the risk of bureaucratic disaster. On the other hand, monochronic organizations tend to be blind to the humanity of their members. Polychronic cultures are, by nature, people-oriented; in these cultures, one cannot cut people off because of a schedule. They must be heard out because they are valued. In contrast, monochronic cultures are oriented to tasks,

---

[30] Ibid.

schedules and procedures, thus relegating humanity and employee morale to a place of lesser prominence.[31]

Yet another critical observation by Hall is that in polychronic, people-oriented cultures, family takes precedence over all else, with friends coming in a close second. Polychronic people will generally try to fit unscheduled favors to family or friends into scheduled events, which can cause consternation to the monochronic businessperson or customer. Should the accommodation fail to be made, however, there may be endless repercussions from the "slighted" friends or family members. Additionally, Hall points out that the degree of accommodation and who is pushed aside to make it is in itself a communication; the more important the customer or business that is disrupted to grant the favor, the more reassured the favored family member or friend will feel. Therefore, the way to ensure the message that one is accepted or loved in a polychronic culture is, according to Hall, to call up at the last minute and expect everyone to rearrange everything to accommodate the change, with a failure to do this being perceived as a clear signal that the other party simply does not care

---

[31] Ibid.

192

enough. To a monochronic person caught in this kind of pattern, this preferential treatment of family and friends can be an insurmountable obstacle.[32]

Trompenaars and Hampden-Turner observe that synchronic or polychronic styles can seem extraordinary to people from cultures with a different time orientation. The ability of polychronic individuals to effectively multitask may be interpreted by monochronic people as a slight, leaving them feeling as though they are not being paid proper attention. Equally puzzling to the monochronic person is the polychronic individual's apparent lack of preoccupation with punctuality, and vice versa: polychronic individuals may be fascinated with monochronic people's seeming obsession with schedules and punctuality. This results from a fundamental difference in philosophies toward time: to the sequential or monochronic person, time is a commodity to be used up, and lateness bears a cost because "time is money;" to the polychronic or synchronous person, however, several cultural values vie with punctuality for preeminence, including the need to give time to people with whom one has a

---

[32] Ibid.

relationship, which could result in temporary delaying of appointments or late starts for meetings.[33] This makes sense given the fact that polychronic societies tend to be high context and collectivist, placing great value on people and relationships.

Here's a list from Edward and Mildred Hall of key differences between monochronic and polychronic people. They argue that people from monochronic cultures generally:

- Do one thing at a time, while polychronics do many things at once

- Concentrate on the job, while polychronics are highly distractible and subject to interruptions

- Take time commitments such as deadlines and schedules seriously, while polychronics consider time commitments an objective to be achieved if possible

- Are low-context and need information, while polychronics are high context and already have information

---

[33] Trompenaars, F., & Hampden-Turner, C. (1998). *Riding the waves of culture: Understanding diversity in global business.* New York, NY: McGraw-Hill.

- Are committed to the job, while polychronics are committed to people and human relationships

- Adhere religiously to plans, while polychronics change plans often and easily

- Are concerned about not disturbing others and follow rules of privacy and consideration, while polychronics are more concerned with those who are closely related, such as family, friends and close business associates, than with privacy

- Show great respect for private property, seldom borrowing or lending, while polychronics borrow and lend often and easily

- Emphasize promptness, while polychronics base promptness on the relationship, and

- Are accustomed to short-term relationships, while polychronics have a strong tendency to build lifetime relationships.[34]

---

[34] Hall, E., & Hall, M. (1990). *Understanding cultural differences*. Yarmouth, ME: Intercultural Press, Inc.

So, a word to the wise: we are probably not going to change anyone's time orientation...this is too deeply ingrained. When we create assignments, we need to consider the difference in time perception between or among cultures and build contingencies into our projects.

Bringing it home

Okay, enough of the lecture. Hopefully at this point we've read enough to realize one simple fact: culture really is an important determinant of how people receive and decode our messages. Our organization provides a unique and challenging environment, because it includes people from and in at least 11 countries – and many of those countries have subcultures within themselves. So how do we develop a communication style that takes into consideration every nuance of every culture we're dealing with?

The answer is that we don't. That would simply be impossible. The best we can hope for is to develop a common voice that accurately conveys essential information among the diverse cultures of our workforce, and that avoids committing major cultural gaffes as much as possible. You can draw your own conclusions about how to do this from the discussion above; or, even better, hopefully this discussion has piqued your interest enough that you'll go out and do some research of your own on intercultural communication.

Allow me to just suggest some simple guidelines to help us communicate better with the field. Since email is our instrument of choice, that's what I'll focus on.

- Remember that very few of our communications coordinators are native English speakers. Because of this, use our low-context communication style to full advantage: provide detailed written instructions, but make sure they are in simple English that is devoid of slang and inside cultural references. Consider the difference between "let's try to accomplish this task" and "let's try to knock this out;" in the first instance, you clearly communicate to the CC exactly what you are hoping for. In the second, however, you leave him or her running to an agency translator to figure out what your colloquialism meant, because in his or her language, "knock this out" probably most closely translates to doing physical violence to something or someone.

- Since we are encouraged to use our low context style, we should also remember that, by definition, that style is short on warmth. Make the extra effort to include little gestures that recognize the reader's humanity − but again, avoid slang and colloquialisms. Telling the CC "you da bomb" will quite likely leave him or her wondering if being compared to a weapon of mass destruction is a thinly-veiled insult...something you would avoid altogether by simply saying, "you do very good work." Likewise, closing your email with "See you later, Alligator," will leave the CC wondering why you are comparing him or her to a somewhat vicious reptile. There simply is no translation for this (and other) homegrown saying outside of English.

- Feel free to copy agency directors on when you assign a task to a CC, but be very cautious about whom you copy if you have to send a reprimand. If you cause the CC to lose face before his or her supervisor, it will be a long time before this insult is forgotten...if it ever is.

- In a recent exercise where members of the home office team and communications coordinators in the field created an email assigning a mock task to the communications coordinator team, the emails from the home office team were uniformly businesslike and almost completely lacking in personal warmth. That is not an indictment of the home office team; instead, it conforms perfectly to the low-context style of writing typical of the United States. However, the communications coordinators almost invariably included compliments and recognition of the other CCs' professional abilities and dedication – again, a stereotypical trait of high-context communication. It would be wise for the home team to take notice of this, as our directness may actually be perceived as offensive if we are not careful.

- When emphasizing the importance of deadlines, do more than simply stress the importance of the task. In the same email exercise referred to above, most communications coordinators included an explanation of why the deadline was so important that explained its impact on the organization and, ultimately, on the sponsored children themselves. By including the personal element while setting deadlines, we take into consideration and respect the polychronic perspective of "people over schedules," yet at the same time we achieve the desired effect.

- Finally, although we have tended to do this in the past, we should be very cautious about inserting ourselves into the CC's schedule to the point of rearranging tasks. We could easily find ourselves placing the CC in an untenable position with his or her local team because of ingroup bias, and we could also be unintentionally disrespecting his or her ability to manage his or her own schedule.

None of these approaches is a panacea to our communications issues. There will no doubt be cases where all the cultural niceties in the world won't solve the problem. We'll have to deal with these on a case-by-case basis. But hopefully, by taking just a little time to consider the cultural implications of our electronic communications, we can avoid making mistakes that might alienate our intercultural team members, and at the same time we just might streamline our processes. It's worth a try!